Restructuring Around Standards

A Practitioner's Guide to Design and Implementation

Terry J. Foriska

CORWIN PRESS, INC.
A Sage Publications Company
Thousand Oaks, California

For information:

 Corwin Press, Inc.
A Sage Publications Company
2455 Teller Road
Thousand Oaks, California 91320
E-mail: order@corwinpress.com

SAGE Publications Ltd.
6 Bonhill Street
London EC2A 4PU
United Kingdom

SAGE Publications India Pvt. Ltd.
M-32 Market
Greater Kailash I
New Delhi 110 048 India

Printed in the United States of America

Library of Congress Cataloging-in-Publication Data

Foriska, Terry J.
    Restructuring around standards: A practitioner's guide to design and implementation / by Terry J. Foriska.
    p.   cm.
    Includes bibliographical references and index.
    ISBN 0-8039-6682-2 (cloth: acid-free paper).
ISBN 0-8039-6683-0 (pbk.: acid-free paper)
    1. Education—Standards—United States. 2. School improvement programs—United States. 3. Curriculum planning—United States. 4. Educational tests and measurements—United States.   I. Title.
    LB3060.83.F67 1998
    379.1'58'0973—dc21   97-45276

This book is printed on acid-free paper.

98 99 00 01 02 03 10 9 8 7 6 5 4 3 2 1

Production Editor: Sherrise M. Purdum
Production Assistant: Denise Santoyo
Editorial Assistant: Kristen L. Gibson
Typesetter/Designer: Rebecca Evans
Indexer: Mary Mortensen
Cover Designer: Marcia M. Rosenburg
Print Buyer: Anna Chin

Contents

Preface

Current literature is filled with debate around the concept of standards. President Clinton's call for standards-based education in his February 1997 State of the Union Address further heightened interest in the subject and spread it from the White House to virtually every home in the country.

It is a subject at the forefront in every school district today. What educators don't need is another book on the pros and cons of standards in schools; what they do need is an objective guide for designing and implementing standards in a way that will meet the needs of their particular school district.

Developed for Administrators by an Administrator

As an educator, I know first-hand how much literature is out there on the controversy of standards and how little exists when it comes to practical applications. That is why I created this book. In my last two positions as an administrator, I guided the implementation of standards without the benefit of a proven process. I have since refined a process that has been effective at not only designing and implementing standards, but doing so with school and community support.

One of the most important qualities of this book is that it is written for administrators by an active administrator. I know the kind of tool that would have helped me, and I developed this book as a step-by-step guide that can be picked up and followed by a superintendent, assistant superintendent, curriculum director, principal, department chair, team leader, teacher, or any individual responsible for or interested in school restructuring around standards.

A Practical Framework

This book proposes and describes a framework for not only designing academic standards but for refining them through a curriculum design process so they will be meaningful for classroom instruction.

An operational framework for approaching the task of standards-based reform is developed through four key beliefs:

- Think big, but start small
- Work in teams
- Utilize best knowledge
- Use data to drive the system

These beliefs, and where and how they mesh, are briefly referenced below and will be addressed and discussed throughout the book.

Every organization needs to begin with a vision of what the organization should look like and what students need to know for the future. Developing this big picture will be shown through the process of strategic planning and stakeholder involvement. It is also through this process that you will see how your organization can identify areas for life-long standards.

The team concept can have a tremendous impact. According to Schmoker (1996), schools would perform better if teachers worked in focused, supportive teams, and more could be accomplished through team problem solving than by individuals working in isolation. I believe every plan or implementation should evolve from a team. The team concept allows staff to develop ownership for the change process. The team concept also delivers to staff the message that they are not working alone. This, as you know, is a vital element because it is known that any success is going to hinge on what happens at the classroom level. This type of philosophy, and its success, will be shown. It has been utilized for the development of content and curriculum standards through the collaboration of curriculum teams. The evolvement of performance standards will be highlighted through teams designing assessments.

The next belief—best knowledge drives the process—should be the cornerstone of all that is done. In our work, every change or reform effort starts with a review of the best knowledge about the topic under study. Once it is determined where we want the organization to be and where it is, the best knowledge about current practices and available resources is used to help close the gap. Best knowledge is used to inform individuals with practical and professional knowledge. The outside research can then be used as a basis for teachers to conduct their own research at the classroom level. The utilization of best knowledge is referenced throughout the book.

Lastly, collect and use data. Data are used to determine how effectively the improvement process is occurring. Data about the achievement of students guides our organization because information reveals where change efforts have resulted in success or failure.

This strategic approach can be a "shelf product" that any school district can follow. Schools and districts that embrace the standards-based movement can make a concerted effort to improve not only the quality of education provided to their students but also to enhance their mode of doing business through increased accountability to the community served.

Description of Contents

Chapter 1: What Do We Mean by Standards?

Chapter 1 begins with a brief discussion on the need for standards and follows with a look at several different ways standards have been described and defined. The chapter closes with identifying and defining four categories of standards that will be addressed throughout the book.

Chapter 2: A Changing World and the Demand for Standards

Chapter 2 discusses the need for schools to organize for success—that organizing for success must be driven by "best knowledge," and that education must occur in an organized and systematic manner rather than at random. Standards can supply the mechanism around which schools organize for success and can help move schools from a current status quo to a preferred vision for the future.

Chapter 3: "Framework for Excellence": A Process of Standards Design and Implementation

A five-step model is outlined in this chapter. It includes the following steps: Vision Setting, Curriculum Structure, Meaningful Assessment, Staff Development, and Improvement Action. Later chapters discuss the steps in greater detail.

Chapter 4: Developing a Vision of Standards Through Stakeholder Involvement

Chapter 4 relates the importance and benefits of bringing staff and community members together through strategic planning to help develop the vision for the district and identify certain types of standards. The importance of this process for local control and ownership of education is discussed. The benefits of internal and external data analysis is highlighted along with some strategies for group processing of information.

Chapter 5: Designing the Curriculum

This chapter provides an overview of the elements involved in the design of a curriculum structure. The elements highlighted include Standards Identification, Benchmark Development, Comprehensive Assessment, and Planned Course Development.

Chapter 6: Developing Content Standards

This chapter highlights the processes and activities that can be used to develop content standards. The chapter contains several examples, summaries, and figures. Examples of standards developed in some different content areas are provided.

Chapter 7: Identifying Benchmarks and Performance Indicators

Chapter 7 begins with a definition of benchmarks and describes their purpose. It discusses some different processes for developing benchmarks and provides examples of them at various points of student development. The need for a developmentally appropriate curriculum is discussed. Performance indicators are also discussed and examples are given. A form for checking benchmarks to determine a balance between content and process is provided.

Chapter 8: Linking Curriculum With Comprehensive Assessment

Chapter 8 discusses a philosophy and framework for linking assessment to the standards. Through the use of a "balanced system" of assessment, schools can measure both what students know as well as how well they can perform. A comprehensive assessment system that shows both what students "know" and "can do" is discussed with a variety of assessment methods and tools connected to the standards.

Chapter 9: Backward Mapping

In this chapter, the standards and their related benchmarks and performance indicators are now embedded into the daily classroom environment. A mapping process is discussed that shows how planned courses of study or curriculum guides are developed to ensure that the standards reach the classroom level and are implemented.

Chapter 10: Attending to Other Curriculum Details

Chapter 10 reminds practitioners that the curriculum process represents more than just design. If the process is to be truly comprehensive, then curriculum development must also pay attention to Preparation, Implementation, and Evaluation. These areas are discussed.

Chapter 11: Aligning Instruction

This chapter discusses the final connection among standards, assessment, and instruction. Now, the teacher knows what the student must know and be able to do. He or she also knows how the student will be assessed. The teacher can now choose instructional strategies that provide the best way for students to acquire the knowledge and skills needed for the assessment rather than teaching subjects at random or giving the same old lecture.

Chapter 12: Leading a Standards-Based Organization

In the last chapter, the need for leadership is discussed. Leaders must move beyond maintaining the status quo and set their organizations on a quest for continuous improvement.

Acknowledgments

As I share my experience in school restructuring with my peers in education, I must acknowledge many of those who served a key role in the development of this book.

My deepest thanks to the staff at Blairsville-Saltsburg School District, where we proved that being a leader in education is not limited to the large and powerful school districts. Some of the practices we developed at this rural Pennsylvania district have become a model for others in the state and most definitely an inspiration for my ongoing work in curriculum development.

I owe many thanks to the administration and staff at Gateway School District in Monroeville, Pennsylvania, where I have been privileged to partner in the process of developing curriculum and assessments through all grade levels. What seemed at first a monumental task proved successful due to the enthusiasm, hard work, and support of the entire Gateway system. Their sincere commitment to excellence in education has enabled me to grow professionally and to share my knowledge and experience with others for the improvement of education in general. Specific thanks are directed to Gateway Superintendent Dr. Wayne Doyle, my colleague Dr. Kathleen Kelley, and the social studies committee whose knowledge, support, and efforts helped to contribute to this book.

I have been blessed with many mentors, most recently Dr. Doyle, who encourages creative approaches to push our schools to new heights. Earlier mentors who continue to influence and inspire me include Dr. Tom Meloy, former superintendent at Blairsville-Saltsburg, who is now superintendent at the Nazareth Area School District in Nazareth, Pennsylvania. I must also thank Dr. Jim Keefe, retired Director of Research for the National Association of Secondary School Principals, who since early in my career encouraged and supported my research and exposed me to new opportunities to advocate improvements in education.

Finally, this book would be incomplete without special acknowledgment of my wife, Anita, for her guidance, understanding, and support of my work.

About the Author

Terry J. Foriska, PhD, is Assistant Superintendent of the Gateway School District in Monroeville, Pennsylvania, a large suburb just east of Pittsburgh. He holds master's degrees from the University of Pittsburgh and Duquesne University in Pittsburgh, Pennsylvania. He earned his doctorate in 1991 from the University of Pittsburgh. He has become a recognized expert in the areas of curriculum development, school restructuring, and cognitive learning styles. He has served on a number of committees and boards at both the state and national levels, among them the National Learning Styles Network, the Pennsylvania Department of Education's "PA 2000 Goals Advisory Committee," and a special committee of the governor of Pennsylvania formed to share successful processes, products, and philosophy for improving education in the state.

Foriska was recently selected by the Pennsylvania Department of Education to serve on a statewide task force for developing academic standards and serves on the Pennsylvania Portfolio committee. He has also developed other training packages for the state of Pennsylvania and received the 1994 Outstanding Research and Publication Award from Pennsylvania ASCD. He is a frequent lecturer and has published numerous articles in both state and national publications. He has been in public education for more than 20 years, the last 10 in administrative posts with a number of Western Pennsylvania schools. He is the author of *A Toolkit for Developing Curriculum and Assessment,* a manual on standards design.

CHAPTER ONE

What Do We Mean by Standards?

Public schools continue to focus on mass production, producing graduates based on schedules and "seat time." Just like the "seconds" and "rejects" that occur in an assembly-line process, public schools today turn out students who may not have reached their full learning potential, who do not meet the requirements of the system. Unfortunately, the students and society pay a much higher price for these failures as compared to the products that can be discarded or sold at discount.

More than ever, schools must develop a vision of the skills and knowledge that all students should have when they complete school, and they should make necessary adjustments in the curriculum. From that vision, leaders including board, administration, faculty, parents, business, community, and students must create practices that will allow all students to combine learning to know with learning to do. That belief, in my experience, has allowed our schools to teach knowledge and skills in ways that replicate settings in which knowledge and skill must be actively demonstrated through performance. In this way, our schools have moved from the old industrial model of mass production to developing students prepared for an information- and service-based society, equipped with the skills for dealing with complex problems to which there are no easy answers.

In my work, we took the approach that our schools needed to change their way of doing business. Our approach shifted toward the belief that we needed to focus more clearly on learning and accountability that would create links to enable students not only to know the rules ahead of time but also to know what was to be learned and to be able to work toward achievable objectives. What we did was change the fundamentals of education to focus more clearly on the learner, build the curriculum, improve how the curriculum was taught, and focus on the role of the teacher and student. This type of change occurred through the development of standards.

The Standards Movement

One of the current problems with the standards movement is that there are several categories of standards to consider. Some theorists describe standards in terms of knowledge and skills; others describe standards in terms of performance on specific tasks. For example, Albert Shanker, president of the American Federation of Teachers, defines a standard as "what we want youngsters to know and be able to do as a result of their education" (Shanker, 1992, p. S11). For Shanker, identifying a standard involves identifying specific information or skills that must be mastered to gain expertise in a given domain. Diane Ravitch (1992) also describes standards from an information and skill perspective.

Grant Wiggins defines standards more in performance terms. For Wiggins (1989), a standard is a real-world, highly robust task that will, ideally, elicit or require the use of important knowledge and skills in various content domains. The emphasis on performance as the critical feature of the standard is also shared by the psychologists Shavelson, Baxter, and Pine (1992), who state that standards should be "based on students' performance of concrete, meaningful tasks" (p. 22).

On the other hand, Marzano, Pickering, and McTighe (1993) separate standards into two broad categories—content standards and life-long learning standards. For them, content standards deal with the academic skills and knowledge belonging to a specific discipline, whereas life-long learning standards deal with knowledge and skills that cut across all disciplines and are applicable to life outside the classroom. According to Marzano et al. (p. 14), a standard such as "understands and applies basic principles of number sense" is a content standard because it applies to mathematics. A standard such as "makes and carries out effective plans," however, is not specific to any content area. Because this standard is not specific to any one discipline, it can be used in virtually all aspects of life.

Other types of standards discussed in the literature are curriculum standards and opportunity-to-learn standards (Marzano et al., 1993). Curriculum standards are described as the goals of classroom instruction. They are used to identify the curricular or instructional activities that might be used to help students develop skills and ability within a given content domain. The opportunity-to-learn standards have to do with the conditions and resources necessary to give students an equal chance to meet content and performance standards.

As you can see, there are a variety of standards. The resulting outcome and one of the major current problems with the standards movement is that the public and many educators do not completely understand the idea of the various standards. I have attended conferences and worked with other districts as a consultant and have heard educators use the terms interchangeably when they speak on or discuss the use of standards. This lack of clear meaning has lead to problems in arriving at a common understanding of what is meant by the various terms.

A second problem with standards has been the turmoil generated over the concept of outcome-based education and its link to standards.

In both cases, the public and many educators do not understand the distinctions. What was successful for me and what I encourage others to do in an attempt to deal with the controversy is to limit the scope of standards used and then provide clear definitions of what they mean and how they would be used to enhance curriculum and improve the educational process for students.

I have therefore concentrated the work of my teachers on content, curriculum, performance, and life-long learning standards. The meaning of each was specified, not only for the teachers but for all stakeholders in the district, so that everyone understood how standards would improve academic output.

The Types of Standards

The first category of standards deals with *Content*. The content standards refer to knowledge and skills belonging to a particular discipline. Content standards establish what should be learned in various subject areas while defining the program of study to be designed for that field. The content standards depict the key elements in the program through a focused and clear approach to the subject.

While the content standards are more general in their design, the *Curriculum Standards* are much more specific and detailed. They represented the teacher activity that occurs at the classroom level as standards are delivered to the students through classroom instruction.

The third category of standards is *Performance Standards*. Performance standards focus on students applying and demonstrating what they know and can do while defining the levels of learning that are considered satisfactory. Performance standards seek to answer the question: How good is good enough? Performance standards focus awareness on whether student work is adequate or inadequate. Performance standards enable our teachers to present actual examples of real students' work from which other students, their parents, and the teacher can learn. With performance standards, students see what a range of quality of work looks like—what is sophisticated work and what is unsophisticated. Most important, they see what makes the difference between the two. Later in this book we will look at and discuss some *anchor papers* that were used as a mechanism for making distinctions among different qualities of work.

The fourth category of standards is *Life-Long Learning Standards.* These standards were defined as not being specific to any one discipline and therefore useful in all academic areas to help all students become life-long learners.

The Path Ahead

The problem, once again, is that the public and many educators do not understand the distinctions among the various types of standards and the connection to outcome-based education. The major task is to help all involved see the difference. Making the distinction can be accomplished by identifying standards as learning behaviors that have a cognitive focus in traditional academic disciplines such as math, science, history, geography, the arts, and so on. It is also imperative that standards are clear and measurable and that they are not applied to affective skills, attitudes, and psychological behaviors. It is the interjection of nondisciplinary topics such as self-worth and adaptability to change that have led many districts, administrators, and teachers to defend initiatives (in most cases unsuccessfully) around the use of standards.

So, with the idea and conviction that standards (a) focus on cognitive learning, (b) are clear and measurable, and (c) are based on traditional academic disciplines, I believe school programs and curricula can be designed to prepare students for the 21st century.

It should also be known and understood that standards are only the beginning. The development of standards is not the only action that needs to be taken, for even the best of standards will encourage little improvement unless teachers and administrators are committed to developing their own skills. School districts and their leaders must also acknowledge the need for change and be ready to support massive staff development.

CHAPTER TWO

A Changing World and the Demand for Standards

I recently heard a colleague and friend address a district faculty on an opening-day inservice. In his address, he spoke about an experience where he was teaching a Sunday school class. He described his group of 25 children as having a wide range of abilities. He noted that, during his reading and his discussion with the children, some of them were listening to every word, others crawling under the tables, and still others talking and doing their own thing. He labeled these various behaviors as the "unevenness" that children bring to the classroom. As school organizations, we are getting the best that parents can send us. The good kids are not staying home while the "bad" ones board the bus each morning. We are receiving the best that parents offer and must recognize that students will come with an "unevenness" or gap in talents, skills, knowledge, and experiences.

Although some students come with this gap in their abilities, schools have traditionally been organized to provide education in a "random" manner that can further add to the unevenness of student development. For example, what some students learn is not what others encounter. To clarify further, let me use the example of developing writing skills. There is probably not one educational organization or educator who would say that written communication is not an important skill needed by all students for success. Yet the amount of writing and the resulting skill acquisition by students is determined by the skills of the teacher. In two fourth grade classes side by side, one teacher might be a tremendous advocate of writing on a daily basis and utilize the writing process to have students compose, edit, rewrite, and internalize the strategies needed to be an effective communicator in print. Next door, however, another teacher may be very uncomfortable or inadequately trained for teaching effective writing and consequently may provide minimum opportunities for his or her students to develop writing skills. When both groups of students move on to the next grade, which do you think will be better equipped? Obviously, the students who experienced writing strategies and activities through a planned and systematic curriculum with ongoing methods to develop those skills will be more effective.

So, as an organization or school what we have just done is to contribute further to the unevenness in the abilities students already have when they come to us. Can it be that some of the inequities in student abilities are no fault of the student but a result of the organization and the fact that education can be a random process for students rather than one that is planned and systematic? In the case of random education, parents can only hope that their schools are designed for the future and that their children will be paired with those staff members who are skilled and knowledgeable about the current needs of students.

Organizing for Success

In an ideal system—one that is organized and systematic—all students will be exposed to the skills and knowledge required for the future, because those skills and knowledge will have been identified and all teachers will have been trained to provide all students with activities and experiences to learn and demonstrate what is required. A system organized for educating students based on identified needs will help create a level playing field for all students and not give an unfair advantage to any student by further promoting gaps in abilities.

For me, the process of designing a school organization that educates students in a planned and systematic fashion begins with identifying standards to which all students and staff will aspire.

In our school context, as defined earlier, content standards deal with academic knowledge and skills belonging to specific disciplines. Curriculum standards are much more specific and represent teacher activity at the classroom level. On the other hand, performance standards state how good is good enough; the life-long standards deal with knowledge and skills that cut across all disciplines and are applicable to life outside the classroom. In a standards-based educational system, the standards drive the system.

In order to function, our organization first developed a vision of what it wanted to become. Within the vision, we used standards to help structure the blueprint for developing a system capable of excellence. In the system, we asked and expected that our staff have no interest in maintaining the status quo. Instead of maintaining the practices that brought our schools to their present status, best knowledge became the moving force within the organization. Research was used to provide strategies for reaching the preferred vision. That did not mean that all educational practices had to be replaced. There were many programs, strategies, or techniques that were effective in promoting student learning. However, there were also many practices that continued to exist simply because "that's how they were always done."

So, in a standards-based system, the organization must move from its present status to that of its preferred vision. In that move, the main questions become: Where are we now? How do we close the gap between where we are and where we want to be? For our system, closing the gap meant developing a clear focus on what was needed. With this clarity of focus we could achieve the vision to which the organization aspired.

Here, we begin to use those organizational beliefs that were discussed earlier. The first belief that standards-based organizations should mobilize around is best knowledge. Driven by that belief, our organization moved toward the preferred vision, committed to using and being driven by the best available knowledge. We were also committed to the desire that schools must provide success for all students.

Action Is Driven by Best Knowledge

When organizing around best knowledge, the basic model for our standards-based organization looked like Figure 2.1. In the model, the "want" represented the preferred vision (the standards)—What are the knowledge, skills, and competency to which our staff and students should aspire? Where do we want to be, and what do we want our students to be accomplishing? The "do" then represented the activities, the actions, or both, that it would take to make the vision a reality. The activities and/or actions were derived from the best available "knowledge" on that subject. For example, writing skill was a desired behavior from our students. Best knowledge was searched for information related to writing in order to plan and design an exemplary program. We asked questions like the following: What does the current research tell us about writing and developing writing skills and abilities? What do experts believe? Have standards been developed?

Utilizing information generated from the research, and working with a comprehensive K-12 team, we were able to develop a district plan that identified a calendar for assessing the students; a mechanism for compiling data; the development of standards; an assessment system for determining the quality of the writing; the identification of the processes, skills, or both, that students would need to be exemplary writers; and a staff development plan that identified the skills the teachers would need to deliver the program.

The importance of this type of practice is evidenced in the following account by Schmoker (1996). He writes about the best knowledge around writing. He reports that while research consistently advocates

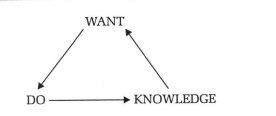

Figure 2.1.
A Basic Model for Standards-Based Organizations

the importance of regular practice in writing, it still gets little attention in the classroom. Many students are required to write without the benefits of well-established practices, such as prewriting and revision, that are supported by the research.

His and other similar accounts support the need for every organization and even every individual to look to the research for guidance. Use the strategies that have documented effectiveness to enhance the capabilities of your students.

Other examples of best knowledge that we have tapped include: issues on brain research and how people learn and retain information; leadership and its impact on progress; early intervention strategies and their impact on student achievement; and organizational and professional development.

Any and all individuals within the organization should be driven by the *want → do → knowledge* model. Whether in a district, building, or classroom initiative, the action should be driven by the best knowledge available. From the superintendent to the principal and the classroom teacher, each vision should be directed by a knowledge base that informs work and effort. With this type of philosophy there is greater likelihood that efforts around common goals will mesh and that organizations will operate as cohesive teams rather than work as isolated individuals in disjointed organizations.

The School Is Responsible for Success

Earlier, it was said that schools must be committed to providing success for all students. All school organizations must accept the challenge of making a difference in the lives of all students. Schools need to look within their structures to assess their values and ask why they are in business. Answers to these questions should focus on helping students learn to learn. Schools must begin to equip students for what is not known. It is impossible to know everything, so students need to be taught skills that will enable them to learn on their own. These types of skills can be addressed through life-long standards. This type of learning has a better chance of occurring if organizations begin to take more risks—to let go of the things that have been traditional and comfortable.

Schools must also help students emerge as whole persons with their egos intact and belief in themselves and their abilities. This will occur only by creating conditions where all students win. It is imperative that schools see their business as creating situations in which all students are served and all students are winners. Gone should be the days of the bell curve, which ensures that some students win but also ensures that some students lose. Too many students have left educational organizations bruised and not served. It is time every organization creates conditions for success and that all students win. Helping all students achieve success may not occur at a fast pace, but the result will be worth the wait.

CHAPTER THREE

"Framework for Excellence"

A Process of Standards Design and Implementation

In the previous chapter, we looked at standards as a school improvement strategy that informs both teachers and students about what is expected of them and as a philosophy that advocates the identification of standards through vision building around best knowledge and futuristic thinking.

In our organization, we realized that standards of the past are not good enough for the future and that it was critical to begin looking at restructuring efforts. Our restructuring efforts focused on the best knowledge about the skills and knowledge required by students for the future.

For any organization considering systemic change, organizational participation is a key ingredient in creating schools that wish to foster an environment of continuous improvement. Continuous improvement should be a fundamental belief; it occurs when staff members develop a sense of ownership in improvement efforts. Staff ownership occurs when there is collaboration and shared decision making around program development. In turn, the staff ownership of new programs and new ways of thinking about education results in institutionalized changes that can lead to improved services for students.

For our schools, the empowerment of teachers and their focus on the needs of the organization occurred through the development of a Framework for Excellence, a model for standards design and reform that became the driving force by which staff organized in teams and accepted the role of becoming change agents while also molding the district's future. The framework, consisting of key steps that continually revolve around the belief of continuous improvement for the organization, is shown in Figure 3.1.

A general overview of the steps in the process follows. Additional explanation will be provided later. For each step, there is a premise, principle, and question. The premise is the basis that drives the action

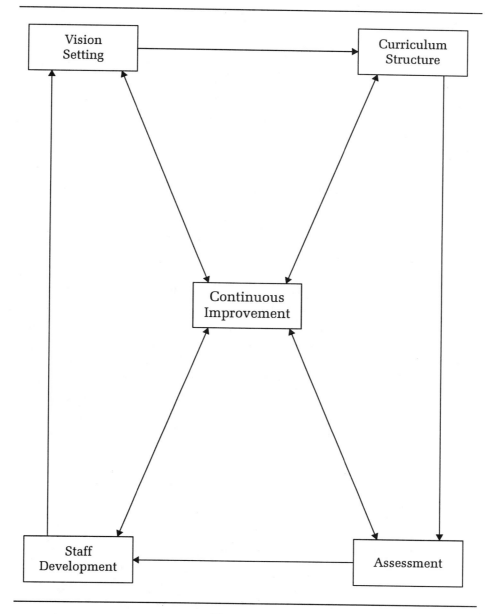

Figure 3.1.
Framework for Excellence

of the model. The principles represent the mode of operation, and the question directs that component of the model to investigate and/or inquire about challenging solutions to problems.

Step 1: Vision Setting

The first step in a district framework should be the development of a vision for the future. Requiring a detailed analysis of strengths and weaknesses, the vision must be driven by best knowledge and create a preferred future for the whole organization and even single departments (see Box 3.1).

Box 3.1	*Vision Setting*
Premise:	Best Knowledge Drives the Process
Principles:	Clarity of Focus
	High Expectations
Question:	Given changes in society, what knowledge, skills, and competencies are children going to need to participate fully in the future?

Developing a vision for the organization, through the use of strategic planning, represents the initial step to improving on that which currently exists in an organization.

Using board, administration, faculty, parents, community, business, and students, the development of the vision should be driven by the best knowledge for what would be expected of students in the future. The central question becomes: Given changes in society, what knowledge, skills, and competencies will children need to participate fully in the future? To answer the question, a detailed analysis of both the external and internal environments should be conducted.

In my experience in the strategic planning process, this analysis of the internal and external environment identified the need to focus on such areas as curriculum, personnel, facilities, community relations, and finance. For example, curriculum goals included the desire to

- Develop content standards in all academic areas with emphasis on learning strategies and the skills necessary for: communication, technological competence, critical thinking, problem solving, group effectiveness, and application of learning
- Continue systematic curriculum revision incorporating content and curriculum standards
- Evaluate all curriculum areas to determine technology usage and availability
- Develop a comprehensive assessment system that emphasizes high expectations for all students
- Analyze student performance to determine curriculum revisions and improve instructional practices

Similar goals were established for personnel, facilities, community relations, and finance. What this process enabled our organization to do was to define clearly that toward which all staff members and students would strive. Random education in critical academic knowledge and skills was replaced with a system that was planned and systematic.

High expectations should be held that all will strive toward the vision. Through analysis of the expectations for the future and using best knowledge, organizations create a vision that identifies the needs of the future.

Step 2: Curriculum Structure

Once the vision is identified, standards identification and curriculum structure become the second step in the framework. Key learning behaviors identifying what students need to know and be able to do are developed as content standards for student performance (see Box 3.2).

Box 3.2   *Curriculum Structure*

Premise: Best Knowledge Drives the Process

Principle: Clarity of Focus

Question: What are the key content standards for this program?

In our organization, staff ownership is promoted as curriculum review and development teams use best knowledge to study the research and current trends as they work to identify what will be expected of students in a single and/or integrated content area(s) for success in the future.

Recall from the previous chapter that this basic model (see Figure 3.2) represents a process for identifying the preferred learning. In the Vision Setting step, curriculum was used as an example of a goal area that emerged. Within curriculum, the skill area of communications was targeted as a key area for emphasis. What we wanted for our students was the ability to be exemplary writers. The question, "What are the critical learning behaviors, what do we want?" was answered by developing content standards. In order for our students to become exemplary writers, we established the following standards:

- Use the writing process to compose texts
- Write with attention to focus, style, content, organization, and mechanics
- Analyze and evaluate models of writing to apply techniques to their own work

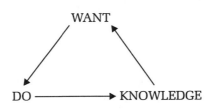

Figure 3.2.
A Basic Model

- Write for a variety of purposes, including to narrate, to inform, and to persuade

These content standards as previously defined identify "what students need to know and be able to do"—the essential core knowledge for that particular subject or skill area. These content standards are clear and measurable. They focus on cognitive learning in traditional academic subjects such as history, English, math, science, the arts, and more, or in key skill areas such as communication, critical thinking, or technology application. They represent a body of knowledge and skills that provides a clarity of focus for staff, students, and parents. The clarity of focus presents a picture of a well-educated graduate. From the time students enter school until graduation, these content standards become the targets at which they aim.

These standards and others then serve as the icons against which performance is compared and are so clear that they guide the selection of textbooks, resources, and staff development.

Step 3: Meaningful Assessment

Once the standards are in place, assessment activities are developed. Assessment of student performance will occur through a range of mechanisms (see Box 3.3).

Box 3.3	*Meaningful Assessment*
Premises:	Schools Provide Students With Success
	Best Knowledge Drives the Process
Principles:	Expanded Opportunities
	High Expectations
Question:	Is the task hitting upon the core of the curriculum—the standards, benchmarks, and performance indicators?

Best knowledge is again used, this time to drive the process of linking instruction with assessment. The evidence that will be used to verify that learning has occurred is identified through the demonstration of the content standards. The content standards are further defined through benchmarks and performance indicators, which will be discussed in detail later. Assessment tasks will be aligned with what students should know and be able to do.

Continuing with the skill area of communication and the focus on writing, one of our standards focused on writing for a variety of purposes, including to narrate, to inform, and to persuade. An actual assessment task asked students to respond to the following prompt for narrative writing:

We all have a place that we would consider to be our favorite place. Think about a place that you feel has a special meaning for you. Try to remember everything that you can about this place and why it is so important to you.

Through your writing, create the place as you remember it. Be sure to include enough details so that your reader can share in the importance or significance of this place. Show why this place stands out for you.

As you write and rewrite your paper, remember to

- Describe the place in detail
- Express why this place is so special to you
- Present your ideas clearly and logically
- Use words and well-constructed sentences effectively
- Check for errors and grammar usage

A holistic rubric like the one in Figure 3.3 was used to assess the students' ability to write a narrative story. The rubric is made up of four components—dimensions and definitions, seen in the bottom portion, and a scale and standards, seen in the top portion. The dimensions identify the critical characteristics or traits. In this case, the key traits for writing are focus, content, organization, style, and conventions. The bulleted items under each of these represent the definition of what each means in terms of writing skill.

The scale for the rubric is represented in both quantitative and qualitative terms. So, student work can be classified within a range of 4 to 0 or of Distinguished to Unacceptable. The dimensions and their definitions are then used to develop standards that show what student writing will look like on the scale. The results from the assessment provided data for improvement and were used to drive and shape instruction.

These types of assessment tasks are used to determine if students are meeting the standards. The assessment can also help to determine instructional strategies. Instructional strategies can then be designed

Distinguished (4)	Proficient (3)	Apprentice (2)	Novice (1)	Unacceptable (0)
The focus is sharp and distinct. The content is not only substantial and specific but also illustrative with sophisticated ideas that are well developed. The structure is obviously controlled and the writer's voice is very apparent in tone, sentence structure, and word choice. There are few mechanical and usage errors.	The focus is clear. The content is specific and illustrative. There is evidence of logical and appropriate structure as well as precision and variety in sentence structure and word choice. There are some mechanical and usage errors.	The focus is adequate. There is sufficient content. The structure is appropriate with some precision and variety in sentence structure and word choice. The mechanical and usage errors are not severe enough to interfere significantly with the writer's purpose.	The focus is vague. The content is limited to a listing, repetition, or mere sequence of ideas. The structure is inconsistent with limited sentence variety and word choice. There is evidence of repeated weaknesses in mechanics and usage.	The focus is very confused or absent. The content is superficial or absent of relevance. The structure is confused and there is no apparent control over sentence structure and word choice. The mechanical and usage errors severely interfere with the writer's purpose and make it nearly impossible to understand.

Dimensions

Focus	Content	Structure	Style	Mechanics
• Communicates with appropriate audience • Information is organized and stated clearly • Flow is sequential • Language is clear • Required spelling, capitalization, and punctuation	• Maintains clear focus throughout the work • Information is complete and relevant • Paragraphs deal with a specific focus • Word choice is appropriate • Correct and appropriate usage	• Ideas are clear • Ideas are concise and well developed • All paragraphs are related, complete, and organized • Original and creative • Complete sentences	• Evidence of comprehension and application of knowledge • Supporting details are provided • Good transitions • Sentences are varied • Paragraphing is appropriate	• Beginning and end are clear and effective • Writing sounds natural and fluent

Figure 3.3.
Holistic Rubric

standards. If that is true, then an important question becomes: How do we maintain the vision of a well-educated student and vary the time element for students to learn and for staff to deliver the instruction?

do we maintain the vision of a well-educated student and vary the time element for students to learn and for staff to deliver the instruction?

Step 4: Staff Development

Next, staff development must happen in a manner that corresponds to the development of the organization. Participants are involved in analysis, collaboration, and conflict resolution as decisions are made on how best to meet all needs so that the vision of the organization can be attained (see Box 3.4).

Box 3.4	*Staff Development*
Premises:	Schools Are for Success
	Best Knowledge Drives the Process
Principle:	High Expectations
Question:	Do all staff possess the skills that will allow learning to change from a process that tends to be random to one that is planned, systematic, and aligned?

Education that is random most frequently occurs when staff do not see the need or possess the skills to make the vision a reality. For school organizations, the vision for preparing students for the future should be a collaborative process made by many different stakeholders from both within and outside the organization. Where the organization strives to go should be defined through the planning process. Moving from where an organization currently exists to where it wants to be should, again, become a matter of using best knowledge to close the gap. Closing the gap means making all of the professional activities directional rather than random. Staff development would be used to provide all staff with the necessary skills to enact the vision of what is described and intended.

To further illustrate and draw on our example of writing, we wanted our students to be exemplary writers. We knew from the research that for this to occur, students needed to utilize the writing process. We also knew that all of our staff members were not aware of all the key components of the writing process or knew how it should be implemented.

So, in preparing for staff development, key questions became: What skills will students acquire through the writing process to become exemplary writers? How do students best learn the skills required? We then identified the corresponding skills the staff needed in order to become teachers of writing, and we provided opportunities for acquisition through a focused training program.

Once trained, high expectations were held for staff to implement the new future in a manner that was planned, organized, and systematic rather than random and haphazard. We wanted all of our students consistently to experience learning activities and skills that would help make them exemplary writers.

For any organization, staff development programs should work toward comprehensive change that mirrors the vision of the organization and involves participants in analysis, collaboration, and conflict resolution.

Step 5: Improvement Action

Evaluation of the overall process is a must. As implementation occurs, ongoing meetings should be held to discuss the effectiveness of the process, including curriculum, assessment, and staff development. We believe that our schools and the entire organization can achieve better results if we constantly examine and refine the processes that contribute to our desired vision and results. Attention to increased standards and appropriate measures of their attainment are key factors in improving performance (see Box 3.5).

Box 3.5	*Improvement Action*
Premises:	Schools Are for Success
	All Students Can Succeed
Principle:	High Expectations
Questions:	How effective is the implementation? What impact is it having on student performance?

The vision-setting process identifies what is desired for students. The success of implementation will depend on establishing effective ways of getting information on how well or poorly change is going in the school or classroom.

The rubric shown in Figure 3.3 was used to determine how well our students were demonstrating their ability to perform various types of writing. Performance standards were established that specified that students needed to reach the Proficient Level on the rubric. The standards were used to develop key indicators for student success, and then the indicators were tracked using the rubric and resulting performance data. The data were then used to reveal problems or challenges.

Using the rubric, we were not only able to determine the percentage of students falling within the performance levels but also to use the results to modify instruction. This occurred by identifying the problems students were experiencing and then having staff meet in groups to identify potential solutions and strategies that could be used in the classroom.

In summary, the framework represents the process. In reality, the staff makes the decisions within each of the steps to ensure ownership and implementation.

CHAPTER FOUR

Developing a Vision of Standards Through Stakeholder Involvement

The first step in the framework described in Chapter 3 highlighted the development of a vision through the use of a strategic planning process. In this chapter, we will take a concentrated look at strategic planning and show how it can be used not only for vision setting but also for the development of life-long standards.

There is no question that schools need to provide students with the knowledge and skill needed for a successful and satisfying future life. In turn, this requirement creates a need to anticipate future needs and trends. Generating a vision for excellence means that schools undertake a process that focuses on future issues, trends, and directions rather than simply enhancing the effectiveness of the existing organization by concentrating on internal conditions.

Although focusing on an internal analysis may seem to enhance operations, the organization loses sight of the competition. Rather, organizations need to recognize and plan to deal with many variables outside the realm of traditional education, instead of simply considering factors within the organization. This detailed analysis of conditions both outside and within the organization is part of strategic planning.

Lessons From History

Looking back in history, one can see examples of American industry that could hardly keep up with the demands for national and international products. Manufacturers focused on increasing production by enhancing internal operations without watching the competition and monitoring a quest for quality. Soon, an industrial society that had been the envy of all nations began to dwindle in the face of global competition. As workers grew more disinterested and demonstrated less concern for the quality of their work, management failed to recognize or realize that human effort must be guided by data and a system of knowledge centered around the needs of the individual.

Parallels can be drawn with school organizations when evaluating effectiveness. Schools must also look outside of the internal organization to see what is expected of its graduates and what the competition is doing. Just because practices have worked in the past does not mean they cannot be improved on or even that they are desirable for the demands of the future. So, if the purpose of accounting for history is not to repeat the mistakes of the past, schools must organize around data that reflect a knowledge of future needs both outside and within the organization. This knowledge should include a deep understanding of learning theory designed around the skills, knowledge, and competence that will be demanded from students.

Preparing for the Future

The push for educational change and improvement is intense. The direction in which individual schools should march to bring about improvements appropriate to the specific school is not clear. Reform reports urge schools to raise expectations, infuse thinking and problem solving skills, eliminate substance abuse, and initiate preschool—to name just a few. How does a school choose its own direction from among competing demands for school improvement? How can a school deal with change in a proactive rather than reactive manner?

Organizing for Improvement

The first and most critical step in a reform effort is to identify and bring together a group of school and community "stakeholders." These stakeholders should include board members, administration, faculty, parents, students, business, and the community. The reason for bringing these various stakeholders together is to provide a rigorous and thorough examination of all school factors influenced by the external and internal environment affecting the school organization. By examining the external and internal environment, a common database for selecting strategies can be created so that organizations can best respond to what will be needed by students for the future.

The focal point for a group in designing a vision of excellence should be the following:

Given changes in society, what knowledge, skills and competencies are students going to need to participate fully in the future? (McCune, 1986)

Focusing on this statement, two types of environmental scanning are utilized. Scanning of the external environment is used to identify conditions and trends that present opportunities or threats to the organization. Internal scanning is used to determine the status and capacity of the organization. Both sets can provide an abundance of data for review and analysis. The data provide a basis for educating the stakeholders about changes and needs in the external environment and about the status of the organization through the internal study. In turn, the process provides for systematic input and reaction from the stakeholders. This mechanism not only allows for ownership of the process but also creates a sense of local control over determining what is best for students and the community.

External Environmental Scan

By looking at the external environment, the stakeholders can be provided with data in the following areas: Economic, Demographic, Social, and Educational.

I have used economic data to look at such factors as changes in the workforce, business types, employment, and economic needs. After examining these areas, the group was provided with a summary of key points. For example, a key point under employment was the belief that job polarization has resulted in high skill areas providing high compensation for those skills and low skill areas providing low pay.

The demographic data looked at population/race, births and deaths (local and state), census data, and age distributions. The social data focused on the family, identifying such factors as structure, income, and age. Lastly, the educational data related national trends, proposed or suggested curriculum frameworks, and survey responses from business and industry indicating workforce concerns, assessment of labor training, and potential training topics.

While key points were established for economic, demographic, and social data, key questions surfaced for the educational data. Some questions were: What are students expected to learn? How do you measure what students learn? Will changes in curriculum, assessment, and vocational education occur? Participants used these and other questions to generate discussion on what would be needed by the students of the district to participate fully in the future.

Focus Questions

Once the data are analyzed and discussed, a group processing technique can be employed that utilizes focus questions (McCune, 1986) to create a priority for what is important to the organization with regard to the external environment. All the external data are analyzed with regard to the following questions:

- What are the national, state, and local trends?
- What implications are they likely to have for schools in the community?
- What are the needs in our community?
- What strategic issues face the future well-being of schools in our community?
- What goals might be developed for the future to take advantage of opportunities or to avoid threats, or both, to our schools?

The participants are divided into groups and an information processing technique is utilized that allows each of the participants to act as a discussion leader for one of the questions. In small groups all of the participants are afforded the opportunity to contribute their ideas while the discussion leader takes notes on the responses. The leaders are then grouped together to generate a combined response. After the combined responses are reviewed for the group and additions and revisions made, priorities are established based on the responses to each of the focus questions. I found from my personal experience with this process that in their responses to the first question on local, state, and national trends, the group identified concerns related to the number of single parents, an aging population, decreases in the need for unskilled labor, and greater school accountability.

Also identified was the movement toward more emphasis on the concept of standards-based education, on critical thinking skills, on problem-solving skills, and on alternative assessment practices, to name a few. *Here you begin to see the emergence of life-long standards through the identification of critical thinking and problem-solving skills.* Remember our earlier definition of life-long standards as learning that deals with knowledge and skills that cut across all disciplines and is therefore applicable to all academic areas as well as to life outside the classroom.

Responding to the implications these trends could have for the schools and community, the group prioritized the need for emphasis on key areas such as communication skills, critical thinking skills, enhanced levels of technological competence, alternative assessment procedures, and staff development. An identical process was used to discuss the remaining questions.

Internal Environmental Scan

A similar process is utilized to analyze the status of the organization through an internal study. Information is provided in the following areas: Economic, Social/Demographic, Human Resources, Pupil Personnel Services, Student Needs, and Educational Data. Again, these were areas utilized in our district. You may choose other areas that better meet the needs of your school and community.

In my internal study, the economic issues focused on the district budget. Both revenues and expenditures were examined and discussed.

The social/demographic data were used to look at present and future enrollment, the types of students in the district, alternative programs offered, dropouts, and suspensions.

In the area of human resources, the data were used to provide information on the experience and level of education for the district staff. The data also related professional development activities for the staff, as well as absenteeism.

For pupil personnel, the data looked at the types of social and psychological services available for students, as well as programs offered by the guidance department and the functions of the district attendance workers.

When analyzing student needs, data were used that reflected statistics for the number of students qualifying for free or reduced-price lunches, single-parent families, handicapped students, and numbers for poverty and teenage parents.

Lastly, the educational data were used to study achievement test results, SAT results, curriculum offerings, scholarships and awards, postsecondary participation, library services, community programs, PTA activity, and technology utilization. Again, after the information was analyzed and discussed, focus questions (McCune, 1986) were used to create a priority for what was important to the organization with regard to the internal environment. The focus questions follow:

- Where is our organization?
- What are our organizational strengths?
- What are the critical issues facing our organization?
- What internal steps must be taken to strengthen the organization?

Again, from my experience, some of the priority responses that emerged for *internal steps to strengthen the organization* included earmarking money for technology acquisition and training; updating facilities; developing content and performance standards in academic areas; improving communications with the community; and emphasizing such skill areas as analytical thinking, writing, problem solving, group effectiveness, and strategic learning. The last skill areas again identify specific life-long learning standards.

Obviously, the responses that you receive from the external and internal analyses or the areas that become targets of emphasis will vary depending upon the needs of the school and community. You may even choose to analyze different types of data or to use alternative questions when examining the topics. What is extremely critical, though, is engaging in the process. More than ever, parents and community members are pressing for more local control of the curriculum and for programs that meet the needs of the immediate students. What this process does is bring the power of decision making and establishing school and community priorities to the local level.

Developing an Action Document

The priority responses to the focus questions for the external and internal environmental scan are used to develop strategic goals that will be addressed by the district. Chapter 3 identified major areas that evolved from strategic planning—curriculum, personnel, facilities, community relations, and finance. Our organization then identified some of the specific areas for curriculum. One of these was to

- Develop content standards in all academic areas with emphasis on learning strategies and the skills necessary for: communication, technological competence, critical thinking, problem solving, group effectiveness, and application of learning

So, one result of strategic planning was the vision for developing content standards in all academic areas. In addition, we identified life-long standards (communication, technological competence, critical thinking, problem solving, group effectiveness) for the district that were identified by the group as being critical for all students if they were to have a successful and satisfying future. Goals were also established for the other priority areas.

A staff development process should then occur that coincides with the district vision and the commitment to student achievement through standards-based education. The focus for activities should be on implementing strategies and programs that maximize all students' opportunities for success in meeting national, state, or district standards, or combinations of these.

Instruction	Assessment	Student Needs
• The K-12 math staff will be provided training related to the implementation of the new curriculum. Training will focus on the alternative use of instructional strategies for using manipulatives, technology, and cooperative learning. • Through a partnership with a local university, all K-1 staff will receive training on information processing, facilitating learning, and teaching learning and study strategies to their students. • In addition to the above, all Chapter 1 staff will receive training in performing assessment studies related to cognitive skills, meta-memory skills, and study habits. Training will enable staff to analyze work samples and design intervention plans to help students become more effective learners. • Analytical/Critical thinking was identified as a life-long skill—select staff will receive training to become future trainers.	• Curriculum leaders from the math department will begin the study of alternative forms of student assessment as well as means for assessing math standards. Recommendations for future staff training will be made for such areas as: portfolio development, performance demonstrations, journals, learning logs, etc., as a means of achieving standards.	• Survey staff to determine interest for participating in training activities geared toward the middle level student. A positive response would lead to initial activities in addressing adolescent needs and program design.

Figure 4.1.
Sample Staff Development Activities

In our situation, a 5-year plan for staff development was constructed. Figure 4.1 shows some of the activities that occurred in the first year (1992-1993). In the same figure, you see a reference to life-long standards at the end of the Instruction column.

Continuing with the concept of utilizing best knowledge, a search of the literature resulted in a district collaborative work team utilizing information from Marzano, Pickering, and McTighe (1993) to define the life-long standards. In other words, what did it mean to be a communicator, a problem solver, a critical thinker, to work effectively in groups, to be technologically literate, and more. Figure 4.2 shows the final operational definitions for each of the life-long learning standards.

Once the operational definitions were in place, a plan was needed to train staff to implement the standards across all curriculum areas. Further investigation of the research identified a program called the

Communication Skills	Group Effectiveness Skills	Critical Thinking Skills	Problem-Solving Skills	Technological Literacy Skills

• Expresses ideas clearly
• Effectively communicates with diverse audiences
• Effectively communicates in a variety of ways:
  – Verbal
  – Visual
  – Written
  – Body language
  – echnological
• Effectively communicates for a variety of purposes
• Creates quality products
	• Works toward the achievement of group goals
	• Demonstrates effective interpersonal skills
	• Contributes to group maintenance
	• Effectively performs a variety of roles within a group
		• Uses a wide variety of thinking skills for managing complex issues	• Identifies constraints or obstacles
			• Identifies viable and important alternatives for constraints or obstacles
			• Selects and attempts alternatives
			• Supports the reasoning and success of alternatives attempted
				• Demonstrates use of materials, tools, and processes of major technologies:
				  – Word processing
				  – Spreadsheets
				  – Multimedia
				  – Graphics
				  – Databases
				  – Keyboarding
				  – Mouse skills
				  – Internet skills

Figure 4.2.
Operational Definitions for Life-Long Learning Standards

Dimensions of Learning that matched many of the operational definitions. Next, a group of volunteer staff representing K-12 and a variety of academic areas was trained in techniques for implementing the program into their instructional practices. Later, after a period of time during which they piloted the practices, they served as district trainers to inservice the remainder of the staff.

The operational definitions were also used to create districtwide assessment rubrics. Again adapted from the work of Marzano et al. (1993), these rubrics were used to monitor the progress of students as they demonstrated the standards across the curriculum. An example rubric is shown in Figure 4.3. Later, you will see other examples of the life-long learning standards as they were implemented through the curriculum and assessment practices.

The Benefits of Planning

The strategic planning process should be a driving force for your district. A long-term staff development program can be designed based on the strategic goals and their relation to the identified needs.

Dimension:	Distinguished (4)	Proficient (3)	Apprentice (2)	Novice (1)	Unacceptable (0)
Problem Solving Definition: Involves developing and testing a method or product for overcoming obstacles or constraints to reach a desired outcome Continuum: Demonstrates a thorough understanding of the problem and uses "Effective Problem-Solving Strategies" to "Unable to Demonstrate an Understanding" resulting in a response that is confusing or irrelevant	Demonstrates mastery of effective problem-solving strategies specific to the task or situation. Performs the steps of problem solving without error and with little or no conscious effort with data that is well organized and appropriately displayed. Conclusion is based on logical analysis of data and supported with sufficient details.	Completes the task or situation with understanding of the problem and using appropriate problem-solving strategies. Data are collected, organized, and displayed. Inaccuracies, but without significant error and have minimal effect on the solution. Conclusion is based on analysis of data and supported with some detail.	Makes a rough estimation of problem-solving strategies by showing a practical understanding of the problem. A number of errors interfere with the problem's solution. Conclusion is supported by data and may be too general or incorrect.	Unable to demonstrate an understanding of the problem because of many critical errors when performing problem-solving strategies. The attempted response may be confusing.	Steps for the problem-solving strategy are completely missing, indecipherable, irrelevant, or off-task.

Figure 4.3.
Primary Trait Rubric

The strength of any planning activity is the process. Strategic planning provides the stakeholders of a district with a process and a mechanism for understanding changed environmental conditions. For you, strategic planning can be an educational process that assists your committee in identifying and discussing changing societal conditions and their implications for your organization.

The district steering committee identified the end behaviors that reflect the knowledge, skills, and competencies (life-long standards) needed by positive, contributing adults in a complex and changing world. A tightly articulated curriculum framework was developed to facilitate the students' development and demonstration of content and curriculum standards that will be seen in later chapters. Assessment procedures, defined with performance standards, were aligned with the standards.

CHAPTER FIVE

Designing the Curriculum

The Framework for Excellence in Chapter 3 identified key components (Vision Setting, Curriculum Structure, Assessment, Staff Development, and Continuous Improvement) for systemic change and staff ownership in improvement efforts. Chapter 4 focused in greater detail on one component—Vision Setting—and the need to engage stakeholders in a strategic planning process that discusses changing societal conditions and their impact on the organization. As we prepare to examine Curriculum Structure in greater detail, let's first look at a model for curriculum design.

Curriculum Design

Organizations need to recognize that curriculum development can be a powerful and visible means for communicating with the community. Organizations also need to recognize that through curriculum development they can fashion for themselves and their constituents an understanding of who they are, where they have been, where they are now, and where they want to go. For our schools, the ongoing attention to curriculum development and renewal provided the organization with an unusual opportunity not only to revitalize programs, but also to give new definition, new vision, and new value to the profession. A thoughtful and comprehensive approach to the standards development process communicated the message that we were a dynamic, forward-looking organization with a vision and a well-defined sense of mission. It also communicated that our organization was committed to the welfare of our students, open to and capable of change, and that we wanted parents and the community to participate in the work of our schools.

Curriculum design, the actual format that is used for developing content and curriculum standards, is constructed with a framework that encompasses development from kindergarten through Grade 12. The format is simple. It makes the work to be done clear and leaves room for the teachers to determine the best way to carry out the work.

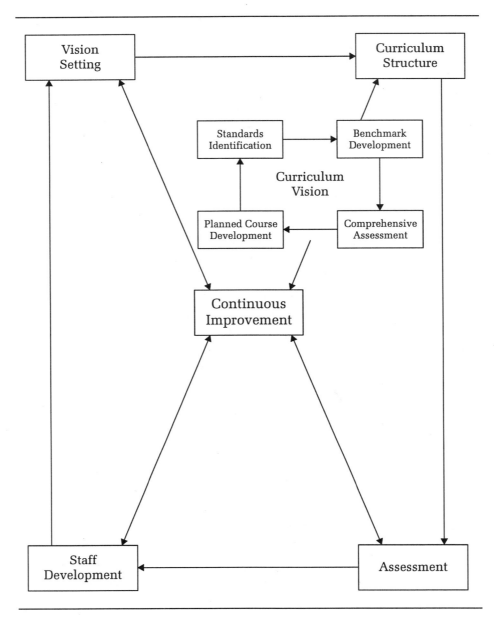

Figure 5.1.
Framework for Excellence

In addition, the design component results in a systematic curriculum structure consisting of standards identification, benchmark development, meaningful assessment, and the development of planned courses of study that operationalize the standards at the classroom level. It is imperative that the design be able to stand the tests of time and change so that its component parts will not be subject to continual revision with each new trend or major thrust in education.

The model is shown in Figure 5.1. As you will note, the model is embedded in the Framework for Excellence from Chapter 3 and thus each element of the Curriculum Structure is also subject to the need for continuous improvement. The elements that define the Curriculum Structure are *Standards Identification, Benchmark Development, Comprehensive Assessment,* and *Planned Course Development.* An overview of each element is next, with specific chapters to follow for each.

Standards Identification

With a vision from the strategic planning process in place, the first element of design is enacted. Key learning behaviors identifying what students need to know and be able to do are developed as content standards for student performance.

A curriculum review team uses best knowledge as they study the research and current trends to identify what will be expected of students in that particular content area to be successful in the future. The question, "What are the critical learning behaviors for this program or programs?" is answered by developing content standards.

The content standards identify "what students need to know and be able to do"—the essential core knowledge for a particular subject area(s). These content standards are clear and measurable. They focus on cognitive learning in traditional academic subjects such as history, English, math, science, the arts, and so on. They represent a body of knowledge and skills that provide a clarity of focus for staff, students, and parents. The clarity of focus presents a picture of a well-educated graduate. From the time students enter school until they graduate, these content standards become the targets at which they aim.

Benchmark Development

Following the development of the content standards, benchmarks are developed as the next element of design. Benchmarks detail the progression of reasonable expectations for acquiring the skills and knowledge needed to reach the content standards. Performance indicators for what students should know and be able to do are also identified for the benchmarks. Benchmarks and performance indicators act as references for controlling learning and assessment by teachers, students, and parents.

Best knowledge, this time with regard to how learning occurs, is used by a curriculum design team to establish benchmarks and performance indicators for the content standards. The benchmarks identify a progression of reasonable expectations detailing what students are capable of learning at different ages with regard to the content standards. This makes the structure of the curriculum appropriate for the cognitive development of the students. The benchmarks and performance indicators identify the skills and knowledge students need in order to reach the content standards. They do this by establishing checkpoints in the learning sequence while further developing a clarity of focus for what will be expected in the curriculum.

Comprehensive Assessment

Once the content standards and their benchmarks and performance indicators are in place, assessment activities are developed as the next element of design. Assessment of student performance should occur through a comprehensive assessment system that includes both formative and summative assessments.

Planned Course Development

The last element of design translates the content standards, benchmarks, and performance indicators into learning; it is represented in a Planned Course of Study. It should be noted here that the content standards, benchmarks, and performance indicators represent the comprehensive curriculum for an academic area. The content standards are general in their design, the benchmarks further define the content standards at various levels of the organization, and the performance indicators are more specific in identifying what the benchmarks represent in terms of student classroom performance at particular grades.

Now that the curriculum is designed, it is delivered through the use of Planned Courses of Study. The Planned Course of Study is developed through a design-down process in which the content standards defined by benchmarks and performance indicators are translated into course, unit, and lesson curriculum standards that represent instruction at the classroom level. Remember from the earlier definition of curriculum standards that they are much more specific and detailed than content standards, and that they represent teacher activity at the classroom level.

In our organization, a curriculum design team developed the content standards—as defined by the benchmarks and performance indicators—into curriculum standards. For example, our K-12 math curriculum has the content standards, benchmarks, and performance indicators defined into curriculum standards in the third grade math course, seventh grade pre-algebra, high school geometry, and so on. The purpose is to develop the curriculum in a manner that will pro-

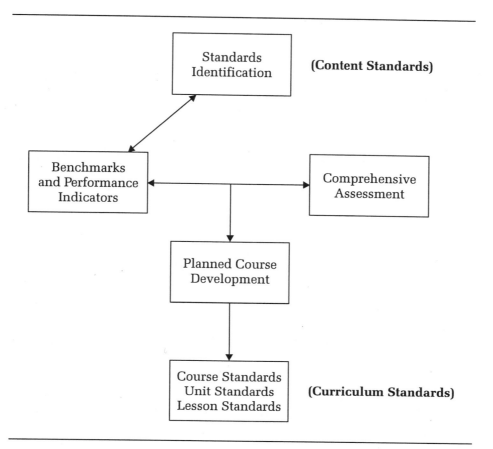

Figure 5.2.
The Design of Curriculum and Planned Course Development

vide students with multiple experiences to achieve success in meeting the content standards.

To summarize the Curriculum Structure: It consists of four key elements—Standards Identification, Benchmark Development, Comprehensive Assessment, and Planned Course Development. The design occurs through a comprehensive K-12 approach and ends with the construction of Planned Courses of Study. Overall, the process enables schools to establish clear standards for what students should know and be able to do; it also changes the delivery system to achieve these standards.

The design of the curriculum and flow of the Planned Courses will follow the format shown in Figure 5.2.

CHAPTER SIX

Developing Content Standards

I can vividly remember a car commercial from the past with the slogan, "This is not your father's Oldsmobile." In so many ways, this slogan is very true for education today. The schools needed for today should not be replicates of the ones that educated our fathers. Rather, we need a new generation of schools to meet the needs of a changing society.

It is hypothesized that when the students of the class of 2000 graduate, they will have been exposed to more information in one year than their grandparents were in a lifetime. If this is true, school organizations and organizational members must realize and accept that moving forward cannot be achieved by clinging to past practices. The "best traditions"—which translates to "what people are comfortable with"—must give way to the "best knowledge and practices" for guiding a new vision of skills and behaviors that all students should possess. This new vision of skills and behaviors will enable students to learn on a continuous basis. School organizations interested in pursuing school improvement can do so with an organization that is redesigned and refocused. An intentionally aligned program can outperform a collection of disjointed and separated activities. In order to build an organization that is aligned and committed, however, there must be a vision of what the organization wants to achieve and the use of "best knowledge" to drive that vision.

Creating an organization committed to continuous school improvement should begin with the development of *content standards*. A systematic and planned curriculum review process should be used to identify the skills and knowledge that students will need for the future. This curriculum review process should be conducted through the efforts of a curriculum review team and a search and study of the best knowledge related to the content area(s) being developed or revised. Membership for review teams can vary depending upon the size of the organization, but should generally include a representative sample from all grade levels.

Best Knowledge

A curriculum review process intended to identify the skills and knowledge that students will need for the future should be driven by the best knowledge that is available through research and practice. The commitment to a new vision must imply that nothing in the current curriculum is sacred. Participants in the process should realize and accept that moving forward cannot be achieved by holding on to past practices that may no longer be helping the organization to improve.

The development of a new standards-based curriculum is built around the need to achieve a clarity of focus for what students will need to know. For many schools, teachers, and learners, this clarity of focus has been sorely absent. Think about the times you left a class or completed a course and never knew what you were expected to learn. Do we play a similar game with our students and try to make them guess what we want them to learn? It can become a mechanism used to enhance control over the situation and the students.

Yet in living life, the concept of clarity of focus is very important. In most cases, when we receive a task from our boss, the task is very specific on what we are expected to accomplish. When we make an assignment, it should be made very clear what is expected in return so that there will be no wasted effort from those involved. Once we know the task, we can begin to analyze what the task requires and gather the resources and information needed to accomplish the job in the most effective and efficient manner.

Clarity of focus begins with identifying the content standards all students are expected to achieve by the time they complete the specific program, whether the math program, science, social studies, or others. These subject area standards tell us why a particular subject is important and what skills and knowledge students will need for the future. For many years, these learning standards were not identified. Subjects were taught because everybody knew we needed this curriculum or because the state required it. In preparing content area standards, committee members should ask such questions as the following:

- What should students know or be able to do as a result of studying this subject for 13 years in our schools?
- What do experts in the field believe?
- What does the current research tell us?
- Have national standards been defined?
- What are the local, state, and national trends?
- What do we believe from our own craft experience and knowledge?

Description

The role of this committee is to develop a vision of what skills and knowledge all students should have when they complete the academic area. From that vision, you must create practices that will allow students to combine learning to know with learning to do. In that way, our school will teach knowledge and skills in ways that replicate settings in which knowledge and skill must be actively demonstrated. It is imperative that we take a critical look at our curriculum and develop a vision that moves from maintaining the status quo to a state of continuous improvement. Only through a commitment to identifying new knowledge, skills, and competencies can we move from status quo to continuous improvement.

You have been asked to review information that represents the current thinking and trends about the area under review. In the next several activities, you will be asked to utilize that information to help formulate a vision based on best knowledge about learning and the skills and knowledge required by students for the future.

Activities will include using the current research and trends to design an exemplary program; identifying major concepts for individual grades or levels; discussing strengths and weaknesses of the current program; analyzing national and/or state standards for their application to our program; extending the major concepts with appropriate skills, knowledge, competencies, etc.; and lastly, developing standards.

Figure 6.1.
Overview

The answers to these questions are developed after a thorough look at the best knowledge available about the subject. Further, you can look at local records to analyze test scores and gather parent and student testimony.

In your organization, you should work hard to avoid recycling ignorance. Make sure that decision makers are informed with current research about what you want the future to look like. How can anyone be expected to make decisions that will affect thousands of students over the course of many years without appropriate knowledge? It is therefore necessary that you take the position that all individuals involved in the curriculum process will have knowledge that reflects the current trends, best knowledge, and ideas from experts in the field, with national data and standards available when possible. Figure 6.1 represents an overview sheet that participants receive on the standards development activities.

Standards Development Activities

The clarity of focus is achieved by conducting a series of activities with the subject area committee:

Activity 1. *Best Knowledge:* Review the best knowledge available through articles and information that represents the most current literature and thinking on the issues and trends for the area.

Activity 2. *Exemplary Program:* Utilize the best knowledge to design a curriculum vision that will represent an exemplary program.

Activity 3. *Big Ideas:* Identify the knowledge or major concepts (Big Ideas) that will serve as the horizontal elements for the curriculum and, more important, the building blocks for the future curriculum.

Activity 4. *Strengths and Weaknesses:* Pose critical questions that analyze the strengths and weaknesses of the current program.

Activity 5. *National and State Standards:* Review and examine national and/or state standards or curriculum frameworks that currently exist for the area.

Activity 6. *Strand Extension:* Extend the Big Ideas developed in Activity 3 to include knowledge, skills, strategies, competencies, and so on, at each grade or subject level that will represent the horizontal elements of the curriculum.

Activity 7. *Standards Development:* Develop the content standards.

In the initial activity, the review team examines the research for information that could impact on the future of the program. Collect and review articles that represent the most current literature on the issues and trends for the curriculum area to be developed. To ensure the curriculum will be based on sound research and practice, you should address the following through your "best knowledge" search:

- Effective teaching and learning in the field
- Major national curriculum projects
- Recommendations by experts
- Requirements of state frameworks
- Standards recommended by professional organizations
- Nature of students' cognitive development
- Content of exemplary programs

For example, when preparing for a Social Studies review and revision, our organization found that the best knowledge came from the following sources: *National History Standards Project, Social Education National Standards for Civics and Government, Charting a Course: Social Studies for the 21st Century, National Geography Standards, Renewing the Social Studies Curriculum* and *The National Council for History Education.*

Review information that is appropriate to your grade level and/or subject. Figure 6.2 shows a worksheet that is used to record key ideas and thoughts as the articles are reviewed.

I have also used expert speakers to address the committee on current trends and futuristic thinking. Figure 6.3 is an example worksheet that committee members receive to record key information from a speaker's presentation. Later, the members are given an opportunity to meet in small groups and discuss their thoughts and opinions about the readings and the presentation. This dialogue is essential for the eventual development of the program. As an example, it was after the review of articles, speaker presentation, and attendance at professional workshops that a social studies committee decided that major changes should be made in the scope and delivery of the curriculum—especially at the high school level. Those changes can be seen in Box 6.1.

Box 6.1 *Curriculum Changes*

Current Program	Recommended Program
Civics	World and American History and Geography: 600 to 1600
Global Studies	World and American History and Geography: 1600 to 1900
U.S. History: Reconstruction to Present	World and American History and Geography: 1900 to Present
Electives	Electives

Later, you may want to consider developing a report on the knowledge base that guided your work. This would not only identify the key elements that guided the work of your team but also provide a basis for any staff development that may be required.

The second activity utilizes the best knowledge that is now available. Five focus statements are used that enable the committee to define an exemplary program that is built upon a combination of the new information and personal experience. The first four focus statements are shown in Figure 6.4. The first four statements ask the participants to describe an ideal program: Based on their experience of what the

Description

You were provided with some pertinent articles prior to today's meeting. Please take a few minutes to again scan that information or the important points that you identified, before arriving today, that would be beneficial for an exemplary program. You should be thinking about the task in terms of visionary programs, effective teaching and learning, content of exemplary programs, innovative opportunities for students and staff, nature of students' cognitive development, and student evaluation.

Notes

Figure 6.2.
Article Review

SPEAKER

Description

Use this page to record key ideas from the presentation that you believe would aid in the development of an exemplary program. Focus on areas that the speaker presents in terms of visionary programs, effective teaching and learning, content of exemplary programs, innovative opportunities for students and staff, nature of students' cognitive development, student evaluation, and curriculum pillars.

Notes

_____

_____

_____

_____

_____

_____

_____

_____

_____

_____

_____

_____

_____

_____

_____

_____

_____

_____

_____

_____

_____

Figure 6.3.

current program offers and after having read a number of articles, heard from experts, and discussed their findings and opinions with other group members, what do they think an ideal program would look like and how would it impact students and staff? Again, you can see how these focus statements draw upon the information from the articles and speakers—effective teaching and learning; content of exemplary programs; the nature of students' cognitive development; and so on. Again using social studies as an example, Figure 6.5 shows some example responses to the questions.

The fifth statement calls for the identification of Curriculum Pillars. Curriculum pillars represent the desirable features or attributes in the field of study. For example, in the area of health a desired feature for the delivery of the program might be hands-on learning and active modeling of principles as opposed to memorization of facts. The curriculum pillars tend to evolve from the knowledge base, state and national frameworks, and major national curriculum projects—once again, the best knowledge that is available to the team. The team develops their own pillars for the area.

The responses generated in this activity are later used for validation as the curriculum is developed. In other words, as the process continues, the group can check back to see if what is being developed models the exemplary program that was defined in this activity.

In Activity 3, committee members again use the best knowledge to identify the knowledge or major concepts *(Big Ideas)* that will be taught at each grade level. These concepts are grouped by common characteristics and identified with a label. For example, health teachers might begin by identifying such concepts as circulation, respiration, muscles, and so forth. These concepts would then be grouped and provided with a label—*Body Systems*. Physical education teachers might identify major concepts to be included in a curriculum—basketball, volleyball, soccer, and softball. These topics would then be grouped and labeled *Team Sports*. Labels that came from work in math and later represented the horizontal curriculum for a sixth grade math course were: Number Relationships and Concepts, Computation, Geometry, Probability and Statistics, Measurement, and Algebra. Each of these labels represent a "strand" of curriculum that will be taught throughout the year at the particular grade level. The team should strive to align the vertical curriculum in the same way. By so doing, the curriculum can be extended from one year to the next. The critical concepts and skills can be aligned so they can be interwoven, reinforced, and mastered without undue repetition. The strands are also designed to ensure that students will have the necessary entry skills as they progress from one grade to another in the system. Figure 6.6 shows a sheet that is given to the team; it describes the activity along with some additional examples of Big Ideas in the areas of math, health, science, and physical education.

Description

Use the information you have read and/or heard to respond to the following questions:

IF OUR DISTRICT HAD AN IDEAL * * * PROGRAM, IT WOULD . . .

_____
_____
_____
_____
_____

AN IDEAL * * * PROGRAM WOULD OFFER STUDENTS AN OPPORTUNITY TO . . .

_____
_____
_____
_____

AN IDEAL * * * PROGRAM WOULD OFFER TEACHERS AN OPPORTUNITY TO . . .

_____
_____
_____
_____

AN IDEAL * * * PROGRAM WOULD EVALUATE STUDENTS BY . . .

_____
_____
_____
_____

Figure 6.4.
Exemplary Program

If Our District Had an Ideal Program, It Would Include:	An Ideal Program Would Offer Students an Opportunity to:	An Ideal Program Would Offer Teachers an Opportunity to:	An Ideal Program Would Evaluate Students by:
• Thematic units • Technology: Updated computers, software, cable TV, Internet, phones • Field trips with no limits, to visit geographic and historical sites • Develop citizenship to the highest degree • Community involvement • Hands-on program • Interdisciplinary approach with a social studies core	• Utilize a resource center • Have a lower student-teacher ratio • Physically explore and experience field trips • Engage in more hands-on activities • Experience various learning styles • Be exposed to a variety of multicultural experiences • Be critical thinkers	• Develop a teacher-oriented agenda for grade/subject level planning • Have more planning time • Utilize a social studies resource center for staff and students • Plan thematic units that use a teacher's special knowledge and abilities • In-district inservice program • Monitor and adjust the program as it is being implemented	• Interdepartmental grading • Various methods: – Class participation – Essay – Content – Projects – Oral – Written tests – Alternative assessments • Interdiscipline (music/art) choices • Group-individual work in a group • Peer-evaluation (with teacher guidelines) • Portfolios • Community service

Figure 6.5.
Sample Responses

It is also possible that the knowledge or major concepts identified in Activity 3 become *themes* that drive the curriculum. In this way, it would be possible to integrate one or more academic areas. For example, a theme that emerged from Social Studies (National Council for Social Studies, 1994) was Time, Continuity, and Change. The fifth grade curriculum related to that theme included the study of topics on the Early Americans and Explorers. This theme can be used by teachers in other academic areas, like English and Music, to enable students to see the connections among the various subjects they study. More detail will be provided in Chapter 8.

In the fourth activity, the present curriculum is analyzed for strengths and weaknesses. The intent of this activity is somewhat obvious. As the new curriculum is developed, the strengths of the present program should be maintained and any weaknesses should be overcome. Using math as an example, a committee found that a particular strength of the current program was the spiraling development of the curriculum. Concepts and skills were strategically introduced, reinforced, developed, and mastered throughout the program. A major

Description

You are going to receive some blank sheets of paper and a marker. Use the sheets to identify the most important areas of knowledge, skills, attitudes, competencies, and so on, related to the curriculum that the average student will acquire after a year of instruction in your class or grade. These are major concepts that should be identified and will later become the strands for the curriculum.

Write only one item on a sheet of paper. Also, write large enough so that other people can read the items from several feet away. After a specified time, you will be asked to post your sheets in a designated area. After all the sheets have been posted, related items will be grouped and labeled.

Below are some samples from curriculum areas that represent major concepts and thus became big ideas or strands.

Mathematics	*Health*	*Science*	*Physical Education*
Computation	Body systems	Problem solving	Fitness
Measurement	Food & nutrition	Scientific process	Leadership skills
Geometry	Disease awareness	Physical science	Body awareness
Algebra	Personal hygiene	Life science	Team sports
Statistics & probability	Safety	Earth & space	Manipulative skills

Figure 6.6.
Big Ideas

weakness discovered was too much repetition of skills and concepts in the primary grades. The students were not being challenged with enough new material. The new curriculum eliminated the weakness and maintained the strength.

In the fifth activity, the strands (Big Ideas) previously developed are compared with information on trends and projections from any state or national organizations. This comparison allows a cross-reference of the best knowledge with other experts to see how closely the ideas align. Discussion, modification, and revisiting research can occur, if necessary.

Geography	History	Political Science	Current Events	Economics	Sociology	Citizenship
Map skills	Discoveries	Voting	Major political events	Producer/ consumer	Cultures	Respect rights of others
Types of landforms	Famous people	Rules/laws	Cultural events	Supply and demand	Holidays	Respect for property
Types of bodies of water		Structure: Local/state/ national	Medical break-throughs	Basic needs		Take care of environment
Placement of oceans and conti-nents			Science discoveries			Community service
North American countries						
Study of communities in regions of the U.S.						
Habitat						

Figure 6.7.
Strand Extension: Social Studies (Grade 3)

Committee members then use the strands (Big Ideas) to develop a map of the desired curriculum in the sixth activity. The map will identify competencies, knowledge, skills, strategies, and so on, that will be taught for each area. A sample of a third grade map for social studies is provided in Figure 6.7. Please note the strands (Big Ideas) at the top of the page and the skills, concepts, and so on, under each. As the strands are being developed, it is vital that they are extended with learning behaviors that are based on knowledge of child or adolescent development and on the knowledge base, and that they represent what should be taught and not what is currently being taught. The team should reach higher than their current practice. At this point, the skills, concepts, and so on, that will be emphasized are identified, not areas that would only be introduced or briefly reviewed. The purpose is to avoid cluttering the map with detail and to provide a general picture of what will be emphasized.

Description

The Big Ideas generated (see "Standards Development Activities") in Activity 3 and validated in Activity 6 will serve as the content "strands" for the K-12 curriculum. In this activity, these Big Ideas or strands will be extended to include key skills, knowledge, competencies, behaviors, and more.

The Big Ideas have been posted on the wall or chalkboard. Use the blank paper and marker to identify the general skills, competencies, behaviors, and so on, emphasized at your grade or subject for each of the Big Ideas. Do not indicate skills or behaviors that will be introduced or briefly reviewed at your grade or in your subject. You may introduce skills and behaviors at any time you think it appropriate and you should review whenever necessary, but for now list only the skills and behaviors emphasized at your grade or in your subject.

Once the Big Ideas have been extended, a review and edit will occur. The review and edit will be guided by the following questions:

- What important skills and concepts have we omitted that should be included within the framework?

- What less-important content have we included that might be dropped in order to reduce the content load?

- What skills and content seem to be misplaced by grade or level and might be better emphasized at some lower or higher grade or level?

- Are the maps developmentally sound—do they reflect what is known about cognitive capabilities of students at each grade level?

- Is there good balance from grade to grade and/or level to level? Are some grades and/or levels overloaded?

- Does each strand show a desirable development from grade to grade and/or level to level? Is there good progression in relation to difficulty and complexity? Are important skills and concepts reinforced from grade to grade when that seems appropriate without excessive repetition?

- Will the maps enable the district to incorporate quality materials from national projects and/or professional groups?

- Do the maps respond to any state requirements, state tests, or district utilized standardized tests?

Figure 6.8.
Strand Extension: Description & Edit Questions

The committee then uses a series of review and edit questions to validate that the desired learning behaviors are appropriately placed within grade structures and to align the curriculum in a way that promotes sequential learning by the students. A sample of the review and edit questions is provided below; the complete list along with the description of the activity for the team is provided in Figure 6.8.

1. What important skills and concepts have we omitted that should be included in the chart?

2. What less important content have we included that might be dropped in order to reduce the content load?

3. What skills and content seem to be misplaced by grade level and might better be emphasized at some lower or higher level?

4. Is there good balance from grade to grade? Are some grades overloaded?

5. Does each strand show a desirable development from grade to grade? Is there a good progression in relation to difficulty and complexity? Are important skills and concepts reinforced from grade to grade when that seems appropriate without excessive repetition?

Our committee found the review and edit questions to be very valuable for ensuring the proper placement of the correct type of knowledge and skills within grades and also between grade levels.

The information that has been formulated and checked in the first six activities is used in Activity 7 to generate a list of program content standards that all students will strive to master. The team should use the strands, or Big Ideas; the major concepts, skills, and so on under each of those strands; and all the previous information from the activities to identify the standards that students should be able to demonstrate or provide knowledge about after experiencing the K-12 curriculum. The description sheet for Activity 7 is shown in Figure 6.9, and additional examples of content standards for various curriculum areas are given in Figure 6.10. Examples of standards that evolved from social studies are listed below.

- Demonstrate an understanding of the contributions of people, places, and events throughout U.S. and world history.

- Explain how geography affects the interdependency of location, place, movement, regions, and human interaction.

- Identify a variety of economic systems and their functions: production, consumption, distribution.

Description

The Big Ideas for the K-12 curriculum have been developed. These Big Ideas have been extended with key skills and concepts into curriculum maps. The concepts and skills have been reviewed to ensure that there are no omissions of key areas and no misplaced content; that there is a balance from grade to grade and a development from year to year; and that content that may not be important is eliminated.

In this last activity, you will use all the previously generated information to identify the curriculum standards for your area.

Review the example standards. Then use the worksheet to identify those that you believe students should be able to demonstrate or provide knowledge about after experiencing the curriculum.

Figure 6.9.
Standards Development

- Discuss the historical development of government and its evolving function in contemporary U.S. society and the world.
- Explain how personal identity is influenced by culture, groups, and institutions, and how the individual affects change.
- Identify and describe cultural similarities and differences.
- Demonstrate critical thinking in a variety of methods, applications, and situations.
- Develop clear and accurate expression through a variety of methods.
- Develop skills to become responsible citizens.

These program standards are strategically placed at the end of appropriate grades. For example, they could be at the ends of Grades 2, 5, 8, and 12. Benchmarks and performance indicators (more about these in Chapter 7) are developed for each of the program content standards so that student progress can be monitored as the curriculum is implemented. Efforts should be made to ensure that no student is left behind.

This curriculum process is quite effective, not only in developing the clarity of focus desired, but also in promoting a sense of staff ownership for the curriculum. The content standards provide a clearer identification of what students should know and be able to do; they exemplify a concerted effort by staff to identify critical knowledge and skills. The process and the final product are the result of what the staff researches, collaborates on, and eventually designs as the best possible curriculum to lead students into the future.

Science

1. Explain the relationships among science, technology, and society.

2. Understand and describe the components of ecological systems and their functions.

3. Think critically and generate potential solutions to environmental issues.

4. Recognize science-related careers and explore areas of interest.

5. Demonstrate knowledge of basic concepts and principles of physical, chemical, biological, and earth sciences.

Physical Education

1. Demonstrate an understanding of nutrition and its importance for health, wellness, and fitness.

2. Demonstrate individual development in swimming and water safety.

3. Demonstrate leadership skills and the ability to work cooperatively in team sports or other developmentally appropriate group activities.

Health

1. Identify the body systems and their functions.

2. Identify the physical, emotional, and social needs of a healthy lifestyle and ways to cope with stress and challenges in meeting those needs.

3. Recognize and demonstrate the ability to apply dietary guidelines to meet nutritional needs at various stages of life.

4. Develop knowledge of injury prevention and treatment and the ability to respond appropriately in emergency situations.

Figure 6.10.
Example Standards

This process allows you to design a curriculum that identifies what you want all students to know when they leave your organization. Now, you have a curriculum with a purpose—a curriculum that is developed with the best knowledge available related to what students need for the future. You have a curriculum with desired content standards that students will be asked to demonstrate after 13 years of instruction. No longer will you have to say that curriculum is taught because everybody knows that we need it or because the state requires it. Rather, you can say that the curriculum is a strategic design for the preferred vision of what students need for success in the future.

Summary

The clarity of focus is established by first identifying what an exemplary program should look like. Best knowledge is then used to determine what students will need for the future. Curriculum strands for each grade or subject area are identified, based on best knowledge. The present curriculum is then analyzed for strengths to be maintained and weaknesses to be eliminated, and the strand areas are referenced against expert recommendations, national standards, or both, to check for validity. Major concepts or skills are then identified for each strand area. These concepts are verified for their appropriate placement in the curriculum sequence by a review and edit process. A list of program content standards that all students will strive to learn is then generated.

CHAPTER SEVEN

Identifying Benchmarks and Performance Indicators

When they represent the best knowledge available, the content standards are complete. The next step involves creating benchmarks for each of the content standards. *Benchmarks* are defined as a progression of reasonable expectations detailing what students are capable of learning at various stages of cognitive development. *Performance indicators* are next generated to identify what the benchmarks will look like in terms of student learning in the classroom. What does the teacher actually want to see from students in the classroom? The benchmarks establish checkpoints in the learning sequence.

Why are benchmarks important? Eisner (1995) writes that the graded American public school system was built on an organizational theory that has little to do with the developmental characteristics of growing children. Schools were organized into grades with a body of content assigned to each grade. Each grade was related to a specific age, and the task of the student was to learn the content at the grade in order to move to the next. If both teacher and student did their job, then students exiting the system would all be at the same place with their learning.

A closer look at human development, however, reveals that as children grow older, their rate of development is increasingly variable (Eisner, 1995): The variation among children of the same age actually increases with time. The result is that children develop at their own pace, and the tidy structure that was developed for school organization does not necessarily match the course of human development.

Thus, what we need is a more sensitive structure that matches the development of students. The intent of the benchmarks and performance indicators is to match the cognitive capabilities of the students with their ability to perform the skills and knowledge associated with the standard. It should also be understood that while the benchmarks and performance indicators are designed to be developmentally appropriate, the variability of student development may still necessitate additional time for some students to achieve the standards. An overview sheet that can be provided to the team is shown in Figure 7.1.

Description

The role of this team is to extend the work of the group that developed the curriculum vision for this academic area. At the conclusion of their work, they identified a number of standards that will now provide a clarity of focus for students, staff, and parents. Our job is to now take those standards and bring more meaning to them through the development of benchmarks and performance indicators.

The benchmarks represent milestones that students should meet as they progress through the system. The milestones can be attained at various transition points depending upon organizational makeup of districts. For instance, one district may have as its transition points Grades 2, 5, 8, and 10. In this scenario, students would be expected to attain certain skills and knowledge identified by the benchmarks at the end of those grades. In another district, the transition points might be Grades 3, 6, 8, and 12.

More important, benchmarks represent a progression of reasonable expectations detailing what students are capable of learning at various stages of cognitive development.

While the benchmarks help establish a checkpoint in the learning sequence, the performance indicators detail what student learning will look like in the classroom. The benchmarks and performance indicators provide the linkage between the curriculum and assessment.

The activities to be completed will include: Purpose of Benchmarks, Mapping or Storyboarding Process, Designing Benchmarks, Checking Developmental Appropriateness, Checking Content and Skill Balance, and Designing Performance Indicators.

Figure 7.1.
Overview

Benchmarks

Benchmarks should supply a definite meaning for the standards and should allow staff to discuss the appropriate skills students need to perform tasks, how students learn the skills, and how to teach the skills associated with the benchmarks and the performance indicators.

The benchmarks also provide information to which teachers, students, and parents can daily refer as they teach, learn, and assess achievement. A list of benchmarks should be a critical curriculum cog delivered to the staff. The benchmarks allow the staff, students, and parents to collaborate and to remain in control of learning and assessment. The knowledge and skills defining the standards are very clear and are up front for all to see.

Probably most important are the benchmarks serving as an aid in constructing K-12 curriculum models. While the benchmarks are being developed, the curriculum design team can simultaneously think of potential methods to integrate instruction and assessment activities that will focus on quality student performance.

Mapping Process

The mapping process for the benchmarks begins with explaining the objective of the activity to a curriculum team. The objective is to develop a "progression map" (Ahlgren, 1993) that will identify the sequence and appropriate grade level for teaching ideas related to the standards. The progression map represents a flow of learning detailing the conceptual building blocks needed to achieve the particular standard. The conceptual building blocks align with the best known theories about cognition and learning. The progression map will identify the knowledge needed to reach the standard. The knowledge itself will be divided into two types: content and process (Marzano, Pickering, & McTighe, 1993). Content knowledge will be classified into a hierarchy ranging from facts about specific persons, places, things, and events to concepts and generalizations. The processes will be identified as skills or strategies that can be applied to many types of situations. What is desired is an understanding of when and in what order the particular content and processes should be taught, and to achieve a balance of the type or number of benchmarks classified as content or process. In other words, you do not want a majority of the benchmarks designed as content standards related to facts. Instead, you want a balance of content in which the students would start with facts and move to concepts and generalizations along with developing learning skills and strategies. You want the students actively involved in the learning process and utilizing higher-level thinking skills when appropriate.

Defining Meaning

Once the design team understands the definition and purpose of the benchmarks (Figure 7.2) and the intent of the mapping process, the members are divided into smaller teams. How the teams are organized depends on how your system has structured the instructional levels. In my district, the instructional levels are K-3, 4-6, 7-8, and 9-12. Therefore, the norm was two or three teams with representatives from K-3, 4-6, 7-8, and 9-12 on each team. Each team is then given one of the standards for the curriculum and asked to brainstorm every-

Description

Benchmarks can be defined as a progression of reasonable expectations detailing what students are capable of learning at various stages of cognitive development. Benchmarks identify the skills and content needed to reach district, state, or national standards. The benchmarks establish checkpoints in the learning sequence. The intent of the benchmarks is to match the cognitive capabilities of the students in their ability to perform the skills and knowledge associated with district, state, or national standards. For example, cognitive development tells us that most students are not capable of abstract thinking until around the age of 11 or 12. Therefore, benchmarks requiring abstract thinking prior to Grade 6 or 7 may, in fact, be setting students up to fail.

Benchmarks provide definite meaning for the standards and allow staff to discuss the appropriate skills students need to perform tasks, how students learn the skills, and how to teach the skills associated with the benchmarks (Larter & Donnelly, 1993).

The benchmarks also provide information that teachers, students, and parents can refer to daily as they teach, learn, and assess achievement. The benchmarks allow staff, students, and parents to collaborate and remain in control of learning and assessment. The benchmarks help demystify the learning expectations and aid in constructing K-12 curriculum programs.

Figure 7.2.
Purpose of Benchmarks

thing the standard means to them. As the team thinks and discusses, one member records the ideas on a large piece of newsprint paper or even on a chalkboard or markerboard. As ideas are generated, the recorder also connects the related components by line or circle. What evolves is a web of information that brings meaning to the standard. A sample web for one of the social studies standards shown earlier (identifying a variety of economic systems and their functions: production, consumption, distribution) can be seen in Figure 7.3. Once the web is complete, the content and process identified is used to develop a sequence of developmentally appropriate benchmarks defining the standard. The description of benchmark design is provided in Figure 7.4.

In his book *Content of Curriculum*, Glatthorn (1995) defines content standards as what students should know and be able to do. As an example standard for health, he used the following: "Comprehend health promotion and disease prevention concepts."

For each content standard, Glatthorn (1995) discusses the development of three to eight "achievement standards" that describe the

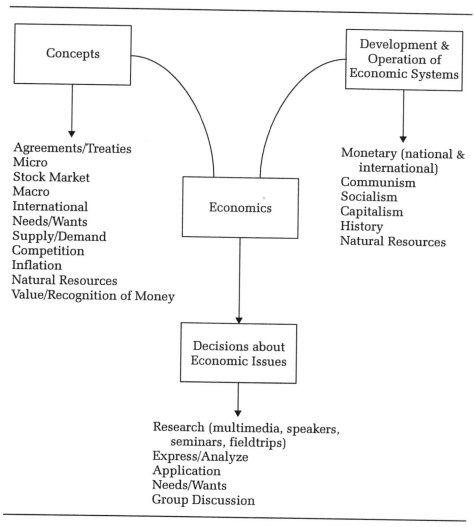

Figure 7.3.
Example Web

specific skills and knowledge that students would be expected to attain by the end of Grades 4, 8, and 12. For the above health standard, he used the following examples:

Grade 4: Describe the human body systems

Grade 8: Describe how body systems are interrelated

Grade 12: Analyze the effect of personal health behaviors on body systems

Mirroring the work of Glatthorn, we decided that in order to be able to monitor the progress of the students in achieving the standards, benchmarks would be developed at four levels. The four levels were the end of the primary grades (3rd), the intermediate grades (6th), the middle school grades (8th), and secondary (12th). By utilizing the four

Description

Each team will now use the map or storyboard created in the last activity to design benchmarks. The objective will be to develop a progression map that identifies the sequence and appropriate grade level for teaching ideas related to the standard. The progression map represents a flow of learning that details the conceptual building blocks needed to achieve the standard.

The progression map will identify the content and skills needed to reach the standard. What the team should achieve is an understanding of when and in what order the particular content and skills are taught.

Team members should determine what students would be developmentally capable of learning at the transition points.

You will be provided with enabling verbs to help construct the benchmarks.

Figure 7.4.
Designing Benchmarks

levels, we created a system that allowed us to track students' progress toward the standards and that gave us a better chance to identify problem areas before the students reached the later grades where helping them would be more difficult. You may decide that other grades are more appropriate. Recall from our earlier discussion that what is important, regardless of the distinction of levels, is that student variability and developmental appropriateness is accounted for in the system.

An example of the social studies content standard with the corresponding benchmarks is provided in Figure 7.5. These benchmarks were developed from the web shown earlier in Figure 7.3.

As teams develop them, the benchmarks are written down with their identifying level (K-3, 4-6, 7-8, and 9-12) and posted on the wall. When the teams complete their standard(s), the entire group does an analysis of the benchmarks at each level for each of the standards. The following questions (see Ahlgren, 1993, p. 49) are used for the analysis:

1. Are the benchmarks not so specific as to be limiting and not so general that no one knows what is expected?

2. Do the benchmarks have a clear sequence where necessary within an organizational level?

3. Does the progression of the benchmarks from one grade level to the next illustrate increasing sophistication?

4. Do the benchmarks show connections with other standards?

5. Are the benchmarks written to be developmentally appropriate, assessable, and relevant to the student's world?

SOCIAL STUDIES STANDARD

*Identify a variety of economic systems and their
functions: production, consumption, distribution.*

K-3 Benchmarks:

- Identify denominations of money and explain their purpose.
- Distinguish between needs and wants.
- Identify the basic concepts of supply and demand.

4-6 Benchmarks:

- By comparing/contrasting, apply a knowledge of consumer decision making (comparison shopping).
- Identify how U.S. regional needs are met through the use of resources.
- Trace the basic development of the American economy.

7-8 Benchmarks:

- Identify existing social, economic, and political problems facing citizens at one or more of the following levels: community, state, national, and world.
- Use research strategies for investigating current problems.
- Hypothesize possible solutions to current problems.

9-12 Benchmarks:

- Be responsible for creating a thesis statement concerning a contemporary issue confronting the U.S. and other nations, and researching the thesis statement.
- Analyze research and arrive at a logical, defendable conclusion that may or may not support the thesis.
- Compose an oral, visual, or written presentation of findings as a defense of the analysis.

Figure 7.5.
Benchmark Map

Using the questions to guide the analysis, team members discuss whether the benchmarks meet the criteria of the questions. Particular attention should be paid to Questions 2, 3, and 5: Does the design show a clear sequence within a level? Is there evidence of increasing sophistication as the analysis moved from one level to the next? Does the team believe the benchmarks are cognitively appropriate for the age level, are measurable, and represent learning the students will find motivating?

Description

The benchmarks define the district, state, or national standards at the various levels of development. The benchmarks match the cognitive capabilities of the students in their ability to perform the skills and knowledge associated with the standards.

In some cases, the benchmarks may be too general and may not specifically identify the content knowledge or process skill that will be expected from the students. They may not indicate what student learning will look like in the classroom.

Attached to each benchmark will be a performance indicator(s) that defines the content or process that the student will be expected to perform or demonstrate. Performance indicators identify what the benchmarks actually look like in terms of student behavior in the classroom.

Benchmarks are developmentally appropriate for the level; performance indicators are developmentally appropriate for the grade within the level. The performance indicators establish further checkpoints in the learning sequence and will later also become the focal point for assessment criteria.

Figure 7.6.
Designing Performance Indicators

Performance Indicators

Once the analysis is complete and the team is satisfied with the progression map, performance indicators for the benchmarks are developed. The description given to our team for this activity is provided in Figure 7.6. As benchmarks are developed, you may find that some are still somewhat general: They do not tell you what student learning will look like in the classroom. While benchmarks are developmentally appropriate for the level (e.g., K-3, 4-6, etc.), performance indicators are developmentally appropriate for the grade within the level. Performance indicators for a few of the benchmarks in Figure 7.5 are shown in Figure 7.7. Please note that the performance indicators are followed by a grade or grades in parentheses, to represent where these behaviors appear in the curriculum. The performance indicators establish further checkpoints in the learning sequence. More important, the performance indicators become the indicators for assessment later in the linkage between curriculum and assessment. In some cases, the

SOCIAL STUDIES STANDARD

*Identify a variety of economic systems and their
functions: production, consumption, distribution.*

K-3 Benchmark: Identify the basic concepts of supply and demand.

Performance Indicators:

- Give an example of supply and demand. (3)

4-6 Benchmark: Trace the basic development of the American economy.

Performance Indicators:

- Describe the U.S. as an agricultural society. (4-6)
- Describe the U.S. as an industrial society. (4-6)
- Describe the U.S. as a technological society. (4-6)

7-8 Benchmark: Examine various economic systems.

Performance Indicators:

- Describe the development and basic functions of the economic systems of the U.S. and other regions of the world. (7-8)
- Compare the economic development of the U.S. with other nations. (7-8).
- Examine the effects of international economics on the development of American economic growth (e.g., industrial revolution, slavery, etc.). (7-8)

9-12 Benchmark: Analyze the operations of the U.S. and its economy.

Performance Indicators:

- Analyze how checks and balances support our three branches of government. (11)
- Compare and contrast the legislative, executive, and judicial branches of government. (11)

Figure 7.7.
Performance Indicators

benchmark will contain the desired performance within its construction and can simply be duplicated as the performance indicator.

The desired student performance related to the benchmark is a key connection for linking assessment and instruction. We knew what we wanted the students to learn. We knew what performance would provide evidence of that learning. Assessment tasks would be linked to the desired performance and instructional activities related to how students best learn the required content and skills.

In an earlier discussion of the mapping process, it was related that benchmarks would be written as either content or process standards. Content standards range in hierarchy from facts about specific persons, places, things, and events to concepts and generalizations. Process standards, on the other hand, are identified as skills or strategies. Our goal was to create a balance between content standards and process standards, rather than having a majority of the benchmarks designed as content standards related to facts.

What we wanted was a balance between content within the hierarchy of facts, concepts, and generalizations and the processes of skills and strategies. In order to determine whether we had achieved a balance of the type and number of benchmarks classified as content or as process, we developed a benchmark classification check. The team used the form in Figure 7.8 to determine how the benchmarks would be classified and whether the desired balance was achieved.

Prior to final publication, share the benchmarks and performance indicators with other staff members for comments and suggestions. They are then implemented with the district staff. Organizations committed to continuous improvement always search for a better method or product.

The benchmarks and performance indicators define each of the standards at the various levels and grades. The combination of standards and the benchmarks and performance indicators that define them becomes the hub of the curriculum. We produced a one- or two-page summary representing the standards, benchmarks, and performance indicators for each level in our organization. This summary gives the staff an overview of the curriculum hub, and they can quickly see and review what is intended for their grade or subject in a particular year. A sample is provided in Figure 7.9.

CLASSIFICATION CHECK SHEET

CONTENT AREA _____

Key:

Content
    Facts–F
    Concepts–C
    Generalizations–G
    Other–O
 	
Process
    Skills–Sk
    Strategies–St
    Other–O

Benchmarks	*Content*				*Process*		
	F	*C*	*G*	*O*	*Sk*	*St*	*O*
Explain the meaning of emotions		x					
Identify the causes of diseases	x						
Perform CPR and Heimlich maneuver					x		
Implement coping skills in relation to stress management						x	
Know the benefits of basic nutrition and its effect on the body	x						

Figure 7.8.
Classification Check Sheet

Standard:	The information or skills that must be learned for expertise in a given discipline or content domain.
Benchmark:	More specific definitions that teachers can follow to assess and measure a student's performance at various stages in his or her school career.
Performance Indicators:	The actual learning behaviors that teachers will look for in the classroom.

Program Standards	*Benchmarks*	*Performance Indicators*
I. DEMONSTRATE AN UNDERSTANDING OF PEOPLE, PLACES, AND EVENTS THROUGHOUT U.S. HISTORY AND WORLD HISTORY.	1. Demonstrate an awareness of how groups influence their lives.	1A. Identify community helpers and their influence on community. (K-3) 1B. Recognize members of the family. (K)
II. EXPLAIN HOW GEOGRAPHY AFFECTS THE INTERDEPENDENCY OF LOCATION, PLACE, MOVEMENT, REGIONS, AND HUMAN INTERACTION.	1. Identify basic topographical terms (e.g., river, mountain, ocean). 2. Relate the importance of geographical area to the community (e.g., river transportation). 3. Compare and contrast differences in communities.	1A. Identify landforms and bodies of water. (K-2) 1B. Define and label landforms and bodies of water. (3) 2. Explain the importance of natural resources as related to the development of communities in different geographical areas. (3) 3. Identify urban, rural, and suburban communities. (2-3)
III. IDENTIFY A VARIETY OF ECONOMIC SYSTEMS AND THEIR FUNCTIONS: PRODUCTION, CONSUMPTION, DISTRIBUTION.	1. Distinguish between needs and wants. 2. Identify the basic concepts of supply and demand.	1. Distinguish between needs and wants. (K-3) 2. Give an example of supply and demand. (3)
IV. RECOGNIZE PEOPLE, PLACES, AND EVENTS AND THEIR RAMIFICATIONS FROM A LOCAL TO AN INTERNATIONAL LEVEL.	1. Demonstrate an awareness of current issues of the U.S. and the world through the use of appropriate resources.	1A. Utilize and discuss a variety of news media. (K-3) 1B. Identify the role of the president and his cabinet. (3) 1C. State the three branches of government. (3)

Figure 7.9.
Social Studies Curriculum Summary (Level K-3)

Summary

The benchmarks create a progression of reasonable expectations that detail what students are capable of learning at various stages of cognitive development, and they also establish checkpoints in the learning sequence. Therefore, they should be developmentally appropriate. Benchmarks are developed through a mapping process and should represent a balance of content and skill in their makeup. In addition, the benchmarks are further defined by performance indicators that detail what student learning should look like in the classroom. The standards in Chapter 6 combined with the benchmarks and performance indicators in this chapter represent the hub of the curriculum. In Chapter 8, we will look at the process of assessment and how benchmarks are matched with appropriate assessment activities.

CHAPTER EIGHT

Linking Curriculum With Comprehensive Assessment

As we have seen, curriculum development organizes around "best knowledge" with regard to current trends and visionary thinking about what will be expected of students in the future. Developing a curriculum vision with corresponding standards serves as a basis for identifying what students need to know and be able to do for success in the future. Thus far, we have identified a body of essential core knowledge and skills. These core behaviors serve as the content standards for the academic areas.

The knowledge and skills (standards) identified are general in nature. Benchmarks and performance indicators should be designed to create a progression of reasonable expectations detailing what students are capable of learning at various stages of cognitive development. The progression of benchmarks establishes checkpoints in the learning sequence. Benchmarks are further defined by performance indicators that detail what student learning should look like in the classroom.

The standards, benchmarks, and performance indicators represent the hub of the curriculum. When linking curriculum to assessment, the benchmarks will be matched with appropriate assessment activities, and the performance indicators will represent checkpoints and criteria for the assessment.

With the standards defined and the benchmarks linked with assessment activities, the written curriculum can be embedded in the daily classroom instructional environment. What the students will learn and how they will be assessed can be aligned with instructional methods related to the best way students learn what will be required. More about the daily written curriculum and instructional methods will follow in Chapters 9 and 10.

Teachers use the clarity of focus they have developed when they assess student achievement. Assessment activities are developed around the benchmarks and performance indicators. Assessment of student performance of the curriculum occurs through a range of assessment categories that include both formative and summative mechanisms.

The Changing Nature of Assessment

Until recently, there wasn't much confusion about testing in schools. Teachers delivered their subject and then scheduled a day to gauge how well their students had retained it. Utilizing a familiar variety of traditional classroom assessments, teachers employed pop quizzes, teacher-made tests, and end-of-unit tests supplied by textbook publishers to search for evidence that students had made progress in achieving the desired curriculum.

Today, assessment of student learning is undergoing significant change. Assessment is changing both in theory and in practice. Teachers are taking into consideration much more than the specific features of a student's particular product. They now assess the age, grade, and developmental level of the student; the amount of progress a student has made and the degree of effort the student has expended are all educationally relevant when making judgments about student progress.

The search for evidence of student achievement is extending beyond traditional assessment. Today, schools are investigating or implementing alternative assessment strategies whose aim is to measure how well students apply knowledge. Alternative methods of assessment are usually based on student performance and can be in the form of assigned tasks or can take place over a period of time. The assigned task or performance assessment may take the form of investigations, problem-solving situations, and assignments that combine reading and writing.

Assessment is being viewed in a new light. Schools and teachers are looking for extended evidence of the level of learning taking place in the classroom. As such, they want assessments that function as an integrated part of the instructional process—assessments that model high-quality instruction and promote student learning.

In addition, schools and teachers are being presented with a broader meaning for achievement. Knowledge was the intended ultimate result of schools in the past. Now, it is recognized that although knowledge is necessary for people to have successful lives, it is not sufficient. Students must acquire other essential skills, such as the abilities to communicate effectively, to think critically, to solve problems, and to be self-directed learners. Stretching learning from content to include other essential skills and behaviors requires more sophisticated assessment measures than have commonly been used in schools.

Alternative assessments supply these more sophisticated assessment measures. Examples of alternative assessments that call for a broader range of measurements include essay questions; portfolios that demonstrate a student's progress through a collection of his or her work over time; and performance tasks and events that require students to research, discuss, and analyze information to solve multiple and complex questions. Students can be asked to write to a prompt and be assessed on the basis of a familiar rubric that is received and explained in advance. Or, they can be provided a prescribed task and then monitored by an observer with a checklist based on an appropriate task analysis.

The complication, however, is that while teachers are being required to have students build portfolios and take performance tests (alternative assessments), at the same time they must still prepare these identical students for standardized multiple-choice district tests (traditional tests) and then report the various results on a letter-grade report card.

In reality, what is needed is the best of both worlds. Different kinds of tests reflect different kinds of knowledge, so we want to assess in many different ways. We do not have to choose between traditional and alternative types of assessment; we can have it all!

Balanced System

To achieve the compromise between measuring students' ability to retrieve information from learning and to demonstrate that students know where to locate information and how to use it in solving problems, an assessment system needs to be balanced. After all, assessment is simply the systematic and purposeful use of various methods of looking at where students are and where they need to go. Ideally, any form of academic assessment will both inform students of their progress and help teachers identify what their students need to learn. In addition, it will provide information to the various stakeholders served by the schools.

Therefore, a balanced assessment system should contain a variety of assessment modes that provide lots of tools for quality assessment. A balanced assessment system should include norm-referenced, criterion-referenced, and alternative assessments. The system should measure student ability to transform, perform, and integrate facts and concepts into situations. The system should take a middle-ground approach, using a combination of traditional and alternative assessment methods.

A balanced assessment system will be able to verify that students have learned facts and concepts. It will contain traditional assessments that consist of paper-and-pencil tests that usually focus on incremental skills that can be graded objectively. These tests are often multiple choice and standardized, and they may be mandated by the district or the state. They have the advantage of being easily administered and easily graded. They can show how well local students stack up against each other or against those from across the nation.

A balanced assessment will also contain alternative assessments that evoke a different kind of performance—an effective measure of students' ability to use what they have learned. Alternative assessments should produce examples of student performance. Performance is knowledge in use. Alternative assessment is an evaluation of how well individuals can do something, as opposed to determining what they know about something. With alternative assessment, the testing tool provides evidence of the knowledge that has been acquired and also shows the competence and originality with which it is applied.

For example, applicants for a driver's license take both a written test to verify that they know the rules and regulations of driving and a behind-the-wheel performance test to demonstrate that they can successfully navigate a car. Together, the two parts provide better evidence about what the driver knows and can do. In a like manner, the combination of assessment techniques provides a more complete evaluation of classroom learning.

The most challenging aspect of alternative assessment is knowing when it makes sense to use it. Designing tasks that elicit a complex performance and promote learning is a difficult and time-consuming enterprise. Tasks should have enough structure to evoke complex cognitive processes from the student, yet the range of processes has to be narrow enough to isolate evidence of the learning the tasks were designed to measure.

If you want to know if students can multiply, have them multiply. You don't need a performance assessment to measure that. On the other hand, if you want to know if students understand how and when to use a variety of mathematical operations in the context of a real-world problem, performance assessment may be the right measurement technique.

Assessment Philosophy

We have established a curriculum development process that organizes around "best knowledge" with regard to current beliefs and visionary thinking of what will be expected of students in the future. Developing a curriculum vision serves as the basis for identifying what students need to know and be able to do for their success in the future. Our curriculum development process identifies a body of essential core knowledge and skills that become the focus for student achievement.

I believe that in order for an assessment system to be both effective and efficient, it must be connected to a curriculum that has established a consensus on what students should know and be able to do. The assessment system should be connected to these clear statements of what is important for students to learn. At the same time, it should be flexible enough to meet the needs of a diverse student body. It should provide students with the opportunity to actively produce work and demonstrate their learning.

We know that assessment has traditionally measured *what individuals know about* something. However, we also believe it is equally important to know *how well* these same individuals can *do* something. In order to achieve this balance between what students "know" and "can do," we felt it was critical to develop a comprehensive assessment system. A comprehensive assessment system would be balanced between assessing what students know and what they can do. The balance would be achieved by utilizing a variety of assessment methods and tools. These methods could include techniques such as tasks, projects, reports, interviews, journals and observations, and so on. The tools would include such items as rubrics, anecdotal records, interview forms, student reports, self-assessments, and a variety of checklists. In this manner, students could demonstrate not only their ability to retrieve information but also their ability to translate, perform, and integrate facts and concepts into real and meaningful situations.

For the assessment system to be comprehensive and balanced, we felt it should take a middle-ground approach. There is danger in taking the extreme positions of all standardized assessments or all performance-based assessments. Either extreme is usually counterproductive.

By developing a comprehensive system that has a balance of assessments, it would be possible to verify that students have learned—both facts and concepts—while also measuring their ability to use what they have learned.

To achieve our goal of an assessment system that would be both comprehensive and balanced, we chose five broad categories that would enable us to establish a framework for assessment: *Selected Responses, Constructed Responses, Products, Performances,* and *Processes* (McTighe & Ferrara, 1995).

The traditional assessment system has generally focused on Selected Responses and Constructed Responses. These categories tell us what students know about something. However, in order also to know how well individuals can do something, it would be vital to incorporate the alternative categories of Products, Performances, and Processes. The combination of all categories would provide the more complete evaluation of classroom learning that we desired.

We have worked hard with our staff in communicating that the key is knowing when it makes sense to use a particular category for assessment. Selected Responses and Constructed Responses can be used to verify that students have learned facts and concepts. The other three categories provide an effective measure of the students' ability to use what they have learned. For the staff, the key question became: When assessing the curriculum and student learning, which category would best provide the desired results?

Formative and Summative Assessments

In addition to the five broad assessment categories, we also incorporated the concepts of formative assessment and summative assessment. Formative assessment was explained as the teacher's ability to provide ongoing feedback to the students about their performance. Formative assessment consisted of any technique used during the period of instruction. With formative assessment, the staff could monitor the personal performance of one or more students as well as the degree of success relative to specific curriculum components. By utilizing formative assessments it is possible to measure student improvement over time. The information received from formative assessments could be used to assist learning, because the feedback received by the teacher could be used to plan instruction based on student needs.

Formative assessments could also be either formal or informal. Formal assessment might take the form of a written quiz or an entry in a student journal; an informal method might be an interview or a teacher observation. The formal method would be represented by documented evidence, while the informal could be considered soft data, which are less concrete.

Summative assessment, on the other hand, was explained as a culminating assessment that could be used at the conclusion of a chapter, unit, or thematic activity. The summative assessment provides a status report on the degree of proficiency attained on the curriculum addressed during that time of instruction. Figure 8.1 provides an overview of our use of formative and summative assessments.

Because the summative assessment generally occurs after an extended period of instruction, it will usually incorporate multiple skills. The summative assessment generally takes the form of projects, written tests and tasks, criterion-referenced or standardized tests, presentations, and other forms of formal assessment that can include any of the five assessment categories. The summative assessment will not only prove valuable for grading but also provide summary reports for students, teachers, administration, and parents. The summative assessment can be used for comparison against state and national standards.

As explained earlier, our curriculum revision is guided by the best knowledge around current research and trends, toward developing a picture of a well-educated student. The clarity of focus developed through the identification of content standards becomes the focus for teacher assessment.

The standards are broken down into benchmarks and performance indicators. Benchmarks identify what students must know and be able to do as they move from one organizational level to another within the school district. Benchmarks represent milestones that students meet as they progress through the system. The milestones are attained at

Formative Assessment:

- Can occur on a daily basis as instructional activities relate to corresponding benchmarks and performance indicators
- Can use both formal and informal methods

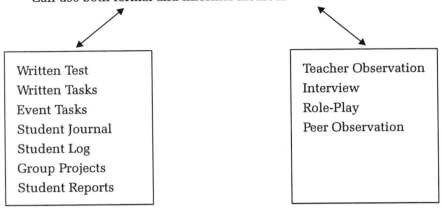

Summative Assessment:

- Can occur at the conclusion of a chapter, unit or thematic activity
- Generally incorporates multiple skills into the assessment

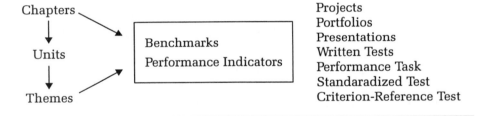

Figure 8.1.
Formative and Summative Assessment

various points. For us, the benchmarks are Grades 3, 6, 8, and 12. Students are expected to attain certain skills and knowledge identified by the benchmarks by the end of those grades. Figure 8.2 is an example of a one-page summary of the curriculum requirements for students in the music program by the end of the eighth grade.

While benchmarks represent the milestones in a developmentally appropriate curriculum, performance indicators detail what student learning will look like in the classroom. The benchmarks and performance indicators provide the linkage between curriculum and assessment.

Thus, assessment activities are developed around the benchmarks and performance indicators. Assessment of student performance around the curriculum occurs through a range of assessment categories that include both formative and summative mechanisms.

Standard:	The information or skills that must be learned to gain expertise in a give discipline or content domain.
Benchmark:	More specific definitions that teachers can follow to assess and measure students' performance at various stages in their school career.
Performance Indicators:	The actual learning behaviors that teachers will look for in the classroom.

Program Standards	*Benchmarks*	*Performance Indicators*
I. Describe the meanings they find in various works from the visual and performing arts and literature on the basis of aesthetic understanding of the art form.	1. Respond sensitively to the aesthetic qualities of the music performances.	1A. Identify music entities. 1B. Justify personal ideas about and responses to the intrinsic aesthetic qualities of the music being perform
II. Evaluate and respond critically to works from the visual and performing arts and literature of various individuals and cultures, showing that they understand important features of the work.	1. Assess music performances that reflect a wide diversity of people, styles, and times. 2. Compare and analyze a variety of music.	1A. Reflect on performances of self and others. 2A. Describe the uses of music entities in a varied repertoire of aural and written examples.
III. Relate various forms from the visual and performing arts and literature to the historical and cultural context within which they were created.	1. Transmit cultural heritage through music.	1A. Identify music entities and assign them to their proper historical period and culture. 1B. Describe and apply specific historic events to the musical works being studied.
IV. Produce, perform or exhibit their work in the visual arts, music, dance or theater, and describe the meanings their work has for them.	1. Perform independently and with an ensemble using various textures and styles. 2. Manipulate music entities into cohesive musical ideas. 3. Refine music skills and competencies in one's performance medium, alone and in an ensemble.	1A. Assess performance individually and within an ensemble. 1B. Justify personal choices and exhibit their meanings through public performance. 2A. Improvise or arrange music using basic rhythmic, melodic, or harmonic patterns. 3A. Perform for evaluations. 3B. Reflect on one's musical skills.

Figure 8.2.
Curriculum Summary (Level 7-8)

So, the benchmarks can be assessed through both formative and summative assessment measures. The formative assessment is either formal or informal and occurs through assessment opportunities that arise during daily instructional activities. In other words, as the teacher instructs on a daily basis, he or she will be providing the students with the knowledge or skill they will require to demonstrate the performance indicator. Remember, the performance indicators define what the benchmarks look like in actual student behavior in the classroom. The curriculum design process also ensures that daily classroom instruction provides students with the knowledge or skill required to demonstrate the performance indicators.

As classroom instruction occurs, the teacher may also choose to assess student knowledge or skill that is being demonstrated. Formal methods for this type of assessment could include written tests, tasks, student journals or logs, and individual or group projects. Informal methods could occur through teacher observation, interviews, role-playing, or peer observations.

Whatever the method, it is important to remember that the performance indicators for the benchmarks now become the assessment indicators. No matter the type of assessment chosen, it should provide feedback to the teacher on how well the student can demonstrate one or more of the performance indicators shown in Figure 8.2 or back in Figure 7.9.

Summative assessment occurs at the conclusion of a unit of study. Each unit can have a theme that can also be defined by performance indicators. At the conclusion of some chapter, unit, or theme, what benchmarks were delivered through the instruction? In turn, what performance indicators in relation to these benchmarks were represented? The summative assessment will generally incorporate multiple skills into the assessment since multiple benchmarks and performance indicators are generally addressed. The summative assessment is usually more formal in nature and occurs through such methods as projects, portfolios, tasks, presentations, written tests, criterion-referenced tests, standardized tests, and other formal assessments.

Assessment Methods

To this point, we have shown and discussed the components of our philosophy of a comprehensive assessment system. We have also discussed how those components can be molded within a system that includes both formative and summative assessment measures. The cornerstone of the assessment system is the curriculum development process, which provides clear statements of what is important for students to learn. The assessment system is connected to those statements, which are broken down into benchmarks and performance indicators.

What we did next was develop a process that would utilize a combination of assessment techniques to provide a more complete evaluation of classroom learning. In this way, the assessment system would be flexible enough to meet the needs of a diverse student body and would provide students with the opportunity to actively produce work and demonstrate their learning. The search for assessment methods to support our needs led us to explore assessment alternatives that would reveal what students know and can do.

As related earlier, we believe that learning should be documented through an appropriate balance of methods. With a combination of methods, we think that assessment can be integrated with curriculum and instruction so that teaching, learning, and assessing flow in a continuous process. Our quest for comprehensive methods identified the following areas, which can be seen in Figure 8.3.

Assessment Development

The above methods provide a basis for assessment. The flexibility to add additional methods is always available. With a variety of assessment methods and critical educational objectives, the guiding question became: What are the formative and summative assessment strategies and techniques that determine what the students should know and be able to do? The standards, benchmarks, and performance indicators represent the hub of the curriculum. When linking curriculum to assessment, the benchmarks are matched with appropriate assessment activities and the performance indicators represent criteria for the assessment. The design of the assessments and their results should show how well the students have achieved what they were to learn from the classroom instruction.

Figure 8.4 shows a template used for designing assessments. The template enables the teacher to select an assessment that is either formative or summative in nature. The academic area or areas are designated. The box labeled "Standard Link" enables the assessment to track which benchmark(s) and performance indictor(s) are being assessed. Each of these can then be connected to the standard that is desired for the academic area(s). The list of "Methods" allows the teacher to choose among several options. The specifics for the assessment are then detailed in the larger box. The section at the bottom of the page—"Performance Standards"—enables the individual, team, or district to determine the performance level that will be acceptable.

Teacher Observation:	Students demonstrate taught skills and concepts while the teacher observes the correctness of the demonstration or response. Other students can identify the skills demonstrated and/or concept being used. The teacher can observe students in both roles.
Student Log:	Students record the results of using a specific skill, then analyze the record to determine their progress over time. The log should concentrate on the critical elements of the skill. Students can record the number of successful attempts in the use of the skill. At the end of an identified period, the data could be used to design a learning curve.
Peer Observation:	Partners observe for the critical elements of a designated skill or concept.
Student Journal:	Students use a journal to record their progress on an activity. In the journal, they can reflect on likes and dislikes, strengths and weaknesses, similarities and differences, and the like.
Event Task:	Students are presented with a set of skills and concepts in a task and asked to perform the task or develop their own performance that demonstrates the identified skills and/or concepts. Students may choose to add additional skills for variety or increased difficulty.
Student Project	Students use multimedia to show knowledge of a learned skill, concept, or principle.
Observational Checklist:	Teacher uses a checklist to monitor student use and development of knowledge, skills, or concepts.
Peer Assessment:	Students are asked to provide feedback to their peers on some defined elements of learning or acquired skills.
Interview:	Following an activity, the student demonstrates or verbalizes examples of the intended knowledge or skills to be learned.
Role-Play:	Students create a play demonstrating the attributes that were to be learned.
Self-Assessment:	After participation in a lesson or activity in which a student demonstrates knowledge or skills acquired in prior learning, the student discusses or reports on these behaviors.
Group Project:	Students design or demonstrate an activity that will depict a combination of skills and concepts within and/or across academic areas.
Student Report:	Students develop a narrative identifying various reasons for participating in an activity. Criteria for the narrative might be the benefits of participation, enjoyment realized, and challenges faced.
Formal Task:	Students identify and demonstrate how they would gather and use information from learning activities.
Parental Report:	Students are given an assignment to practice a particular skill. The students are asked to return a report in which a parent identifies the extent to which the student practiced the skill.
Written Test:	Comprehensive assessment to determine the degree to which students know the information, can use it appropriately in given situations, can apply it in new situations, and can modify it to meet specific goals.

Figure 8.3.
Assessment Methods

Assessment Type: _____ Formative _____ Summative

Academic Area(s):

Standard Link
Program Standard(s) _____
Benchmark(s) _____
Performance Indicator(s) _____

	Methods
	Teacher Observation
	Student Log
	Peer Observation
	Student Journal
	Event Task
	Student Project
	Observational Checklist
	Peer Assessment
	Interview
	Role-Playing
	Anecdotal Comments
	Student Self-Assessment
	Group Project
	Student Report
	Formal Task
	Parental Report
	Written Test
	Other

Performance Standards:

Figure 8.4.
Assessment System Template

Figures 8.5 and 8.6 provide examples of a formative and a summative assessment as they relate to Standard II from the social studies curriculum discussed in Chapter 7 and depicted Figure 7.9. The formative assessment involves students maintaining a journal. The Standard Link boxes in Figures 8.5 and 8.6 show the elements of the curriculum that are addressed.

The summative assessment addresses a different benchmark and performance indicator for the same standard. In this case, the assessment is a project, and you can easily see how it could also be used for integrating other disciplines—Language Arts as well as life-long learning standards like communication skills and technological literacy skills.

Not only will the student demonstrate knowledge of social studies/topographical terms (see Figure 8.5), but will develop written and oral communication skills through writing a tall tale and providing an oral presentation. The word processing of the paper will also enhance technology skills.

In Figure 8.7 another example is provided, this time in the area of music. As you can see, this is a summative assessment that relates to multiple benchmarks and performance indicators. The performance indicators are the same as the assessment indicators listed. Again, we are able to validate that what the curriculum addressed is what is now being assessed. The method chosen is an Event Task. The task itself involves the student taking on the role of a critic for MTV. As a critic, the student is to review a new recording and write a review based on the guidelines provided. Figure 8.8 provides a rubric that accompanies the assessment. The rubric is characterized by three dimensions: format, stance, and justification. These dimensions represent the primary characteristics or traits that identify essential attributes of the desired performance. As you can see, they also relate to the assessment indicators.

The development of the assessment system then involves looking at each of the benchmarks and determining the best way to assess them. In some cases, a traditional method can be used. In others, it is necessary to use alternative methods. As in Figure 8.7, corresponding tools are necessary. In that example, a rubric was relevant. For other assessments, a corresponding checklist like the one shown in Figure 8.9 might be used. Such a checklist could be used for gathering formative assessment data as they relate to "Standard IV, Benchmark 3, and Performance Indicator 3A" in Figure 8.2. Other types of assessment tools could be observation sheets, peer assessment forms, self-assessment forms, anecdotal records, and more. An example of one of the various tools is shown in Figure 8.10.

Throughout our school system, assessment is integrated with curriculum and instruction so that teaching, learning, and assessing are a continuous process. By documenting and evaluating student work over time, our teachers obtain information for understanding student progress in ways that can guide future instruction.

Assessment Type: _____ Formative   X Summative

Academic Area(s): Social Studies

Standard Link
Program Standard(s)   II
Benchmark(s)   II, 1
Performance Indicator(s) 1B

	Methods
Student Project: Each student is to select an existing geographical feature in the United States (body of water, river, mountain range, desert, etc.). After selecting the feature, they will write about the creation of a geographical feature by a main character (folk hero) who possesses supernatural powers, and will give the correct name and location of the geographical feature. They should draft and revise their work as necessary. When they are satisfied with their work, they produce a final draft utilizing a word-processing program and provide colors and illustrations to go with the text. Each student's invention of a tall tale explaining how a geographical feature was created will be presented to the class. **Expectations:** • Format is neat and orderly, organized and easy to follow, complete and accurate • Sentences are complete with correct mechanics • Appropriate art elements are used (lines, shapes, color, points, texture, empty space, etc.) • Directions were followed **Assessment Indicator:** Define and label landforms and bodies of water.	Teacher Observation Student Log Peer Observation Student Journal Event Task Student Project Observational Checklist Peer Assessment Interview Role-Playing Anecdotal Comments Student Self-Assessment Group Project Student Report Formal Task Parental Report Written Test Other

Performance Standards:

Figure 8.5.
Assessment System

Assessment Type: __X__ **Formative** _____ **Summative**

Academic Area(s): Social Studies

Standard Link	
Program Standard(s)	II
Benchmark(s)	II, 3
Performance Indicator(s)	3A

Student Journal:

As the class studies and discusses communities, each student will compile information in a journal. The journal will include information about the community, including: businesses, manufacturing, schools, effects of geography, history, and when possible how the community relates to the state, nation, and world. The journal will also include a map of the communities with legend and relevant illustrations.

Specific Expectations:

- Journal accurately based on researched information
- Maps neatly and accurately drawn
- Included at least three illustrations

General Expectations:

- Neat and orderly, complete and accurate
- Followed format, organized and easy to follow
- Sentences complete
- Correct mechanics: spelling, capitalization, punctuation

Assessment Indicator:

- Identify urban, rural, and suburban communities.

Methods

Teacher Observation
Student Log
Peer Observation
Student Journal
Event Task
Student Project
Observational Checklist
Peer Assessment
Interview
Role-Playing
Anecdotal Comments
Student Self-Assessment
Group Project
Student Report
Formal Task
Parental Report
Written Test
Other

Performance Standards:

Figure 8.6.
Assessment System

Assessment Type: _____ Formative __X__ Summative

Academic Area(s):

Standard Link	
Program Standard(s)	I, II
Benchmark(s)	I:1, II: 1-2
Performance Indicator(s)	1:1a-b, II:1a,2a

	Methods

Event Task:

You have just been hired by MTV to serve as a music critic. Your first assignment is to review a new recording. In writing your review, you should use the following guidelines:

- Base your review on the merits of the recording as compared with the best of its kind.

- Take a clear stance—either positive or negative. Make it clear to the reader where you stand and why.

- The justification of your opinion must be specific. Avoid vague comments such as "it's good."

- Format your review in three paragraphs:

  - Paragraph 1: identify the recording artist; state your opinion

  - Paragraph 2: justify your opinion citing specific examples

  - Paragraph 3: summarize

Assessment Indicators:

- Justify music entities.

- Justify personal ideas and responses about the intrinsic aesthetic qualities of the music being performed.

- Reflect on the performance of self and others.

- Describe the use of music entities in a varied repertoire of aural and written examples.

Methods:

Teacher Observation
Student Log
Peer Observation
Student Journal
Event Task
Student Project
Observational Checklist
Peer Assessment
Interview
Role-Playing
Anecdotal Comments
Student Self-Assessment
Group Project
Student Report
Formal Task
Parental Report
Written Test
Other

Performance Standards:

Figure 8.7.
Assessment System

Distinguished (4)	Proficient (3)	Apprentice (2)	Novice (1)	Unacceptable (0)
Demonstrates a complete understanding of the format procedure in each paragraph with identified elements. Provides a positive or negative response using music entity to reflect on the performance while stating an opinion and examples. The opinion and examples are insightful and even innovative.	Demonstrates an understanding of the format procedures and each paragraph contains the identified elements. Provides a positive or negative response using music entity to reflect on the performance while stating an opinion and using examples. The examples used to justify opinions are somewhat vague and lacking clarity.	Demonstrates an understanding of the format procedure and each paragraph contains the identified elements. Provides a positive or negative response but the opinion is not clear and the justification is vague.	Format contains the three desired paragraphs but did not contain the required elements. The opinion is missing and the examples are without justification.	Format contains less than the three desired paragraphs. The review contains some of the desired elements but the response is generally off-task.

Dimensions

Format	Clear Stance	Justification

• Three paragraphs
  – Identifies recording and artist with stated opinion
  – Justifies opinion with specific examples
  – Summarizes
	• Takes a positive or negative view of the work
	• Makes stance clear to the reader
	• States reasons for view
		• Justification for opinion is specific
		• Avoids vague comments

Figure 8.8.
Holistic Rubric

Name: _____

Class: _____

Year: _____

ACTIVITY: *Flute Embouchure*	Date		Date		Date	
	Demonstrates Competence	*Needs Improvement*	*Demonstrates Competence*	*Needs Improvement*	*Demonstrates Competence*	*Needs Improvement*
Flute parallel with line of lips						
Aperture in lips centered in side-to-side relationship with embouchure hole						
Proper amount of embouchure hole covered by lower lip						
Size and shape of aperture in lips correct						
Airstream properly directed						
Direction of airstream controlled by lips and lower jaw						
Corners of mouth pulled back slightly						

Figure 8.9.
Checklist

Name: _____

Class: _____

Year: _____

_____ Peer Observation
_____ Observation
_____ Peer Assessment
_____ Self-Assessment

TASK _____

_____

Demonstrated	How

Figure 8.10.
Assessment Tool

Summary

An assessment system should be connected to clear statements of what is important for students to learn (Benchmarks and Performance Indicators). It should be developed with an appropriate balance of methods that includes observation and interviews, projects and tasks, experiments, tests, performances and exhibitions, audio and video tapes, portfolios, and journals. All of the methods and tools utilized should be chosen in the context of a comprehensive and balanced system that derives from formative and summative measures. A balance of assessment measures enables the system to be flexible enough to meet the needs of a diverse student body while still providing useful and accurate information about student learning.

CHAPTER NINE

Backward Mapping

With the content standards, benchmarks, and performance indicators now in place and linked with assessment activities, you are ready to continue with the remainder of the curriculum development process. What remains is to give the content standards (as defined by the benchmarks and performance indicators) more meaning at the classroom level. An overview sheet for the curriculum development team is provided in Figure 9.1.

The illustration at the end of Chapter 5 is repeated here for convenient review (see Figure 9.2). Meaning at the classroom level represents the design of *curriculum standards* through the development of a *Planned Course of Study.* Using the content standards, small teams of teachers work individually at their particular grade level or with their particular course to develop a Planned Course of Study. A flowchart for the elements contained in the Planned Course is shown in Figure 9.3. The definitions for each element are given in Figure 9.4.

The development of the Planned Course is accomplished through a process called *backward mapping.* The backward mapping process enables the content standards to be translated to the classroom level in the form of corresponding curriculum standards through the design of course, unit, and lesson standards. A "course" would be defined as sixth-grade math or calculus. A "unit" could be a horizontal component of instruction in that course occurring during the year, or it could be a theme that integrates one or more other academic disciplines. A unit of instruction in the sixth-grade course would be measurement and a theme might be People, Places, and Environment. A "lesson" would be daily activities that occur in the classroom. Each lesson relates to one of the units or themes. Each unit or theme relates to some aspect of the course. At each lower level, the wording and meaning of the curriculum standards become increasingly more specific and measurable. The clarity of focus needed to facilitate students' learning is achieved.

The team's role is to complete the development of the curriculum. To date, a curriculum vision has been established that identifies a number of standards that provide a clarity of focus for students, staff, and parents. Benchmarks representing milestones that students should meet as they progress through the system have been established. Performance indicators describing what student performance should look like in the classroom with regard to those benchmarks have been developed, as well as assessment activities for the benchmarks.

The benchmarks and performance indicators now define each of the standards at the various levels and grades. Next, ensure that the intent of the benchmarks and performance indicators are embedded into the taught curriculum. To do this, utilize a "backward mapping" process. The benchmarks and performance indicators representing the hub of the curriculum will be further translated into a planned course of study for a particular grade or subject.

The activities to be completed will include: Philosophy and Beliefs, Course Standards, Unit Standards, Lesson Standards, Content and Skills, Instructional Methods, Materials/Resources, Core Activities, Enrichment, and Reteaching.

Figure 9.1.
Overview

Course Standards

Each team member starts with the course standards. The description for this activity is shown in Figure 9.5. Looking at what would be expected from all students with regard to the content standards—benchmarks and performance indicators at the end of their particular level (e.g., K-2, 3-5, 6-8, 9-12), what would the students accomplish at the end of their course?

The Big Ideas that were previously developed for each grade level or subject are beneficial for this process. As you may recall, this was the third activity of the curriculum review team previously discussed in Chapter 6; these Big Ideas can now represent strands in the curriculum. Because these strands represent key horizontal components of the curriculum, they can help to guide the development of what would be expected from students by the end of the year. Recall the Big Ideas in the third grade social studies in Figure 6.7. The major areas to be covered in the third grade course are: Geography, History, Political Science, Current Events, Economics, Sociology, and Citizenship.

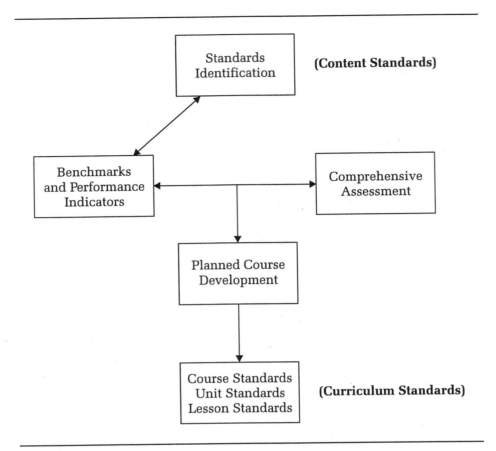

Figure 9.2.
The Design of Curriculum and Planned Course Development

In other words, by the end of the year, students in third grade social studies will experience instructional activities in each of those areas. Below are the course standards that are expected from the third grade students:

1. Illustrate and explain basic concepts of Geography.

2. Generalize basic concepts of Economics.

3. Summarize the basic concepts of Sociology.

4. Restate current event issues of the United States and the world.

5. Recognize the basic structure of the U.S. government.

6. Differentiate cultural and institutional groups.

7. Demonstrate social skills.

You can readily see the relationship between the Big Ideas (strands) and the course standards. In turn, each of the above curriculum standards relates to the content standards for the social studies program. The following represent a few of the corresponding content standards that we identified back in Chapter 6.

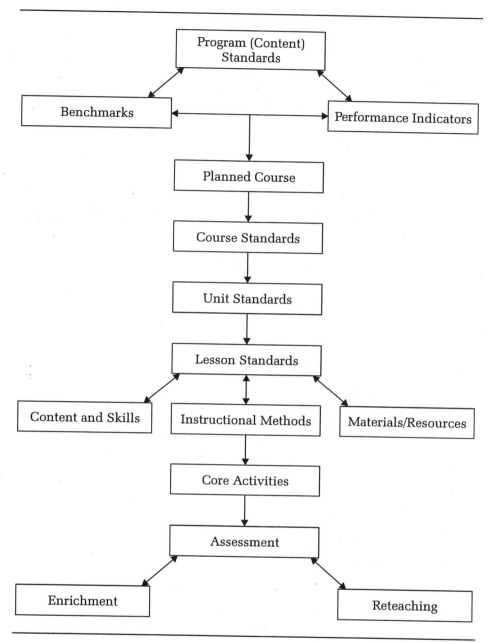

Figure 9.3.
Planned Course Flowchart
SOURCE: Foriska (1997). Developed by Terry J. Foriska and Kathleen Kelley.

- Explain how geography affects the interdependency of location, place, movement, regions, and human interaction.
- Identify a variety of economic systems and their functions: production, consumption, distribution.
- Discuss the historical development of government and its evolving function in contemporary U.S. and world society.
- Identify and describe cultural similarities and differences.

- **Program (Content) Standards:** The general skills/abilities a student must have demonstrated in order to complete the area of study successfully.
- **Benchmarks:** Specific skills/abilities developed by the end of predetermined organizational levels.
- **Performance Indicators:** Student behaviors assessed by teachers to validate the achieved standards.
- **Planned Course:** Instruction based on a written plan that consists of standards to be achieved by students, content and estimated instructional time, procedures for assessment, and the relationship of the standards to those identified in the district strategic plan as well as other planned courses.
- **Course Standards:** Content and skills relative to a specific grade level or content area.
- **Unit Standards:** Subjects, topics, or themes contained in a specific course.
- **Lesson Standards:** Specific student behaviors for meeting unit standards.
- **Content/Skills:** What students need to know or be able to do that will enable them to achieve a standard for the grade, subject, or level.
- **Instructional Methods:** Techniques for delivering the content and/or skills needed for the subject, grade, or level.
- **Core Activities:** Instructional activities that can be designed and implemented and that enable students to acquire the knowledge and/or skills to meet the standard.
- **Assessment:** A comprehensive system designed to maintain a balance between assessing what students know and what they can do.
- **Enrichment Activities:** Extension and expansion of skills and content for those students who demonstrate performance of the standards before or after initial instruction.
- **Reteaching Activities:** Variation of methods necessary for students to achieve the standards after initial assessments.

Figure 9.4.
Definitions

Each of the course standards relates to the content standards for the program. Everything that the student will learn in a grade or course will lead to the desired content standards for the program and the corresponding benchmarks and performance indicators for the appropriate level. Additional examples of course standards are provided

Description

The program standards, benchmarks, and performance indicators represent the hub of the program. You are now going to begin a "backward mapping" or "design down" process whereby the program standards, benchmarks, and performance indicators will be translated into course, unit, and lesson standards for a particular grade and/or level.

Start with the course standards. What will be expected from all students with regard to the program standards, benchmarks, and performance indicators at the end of your particular level (K-3, 4-6, 7-8, 9-12)? Then, what will the students accomplish at the end of your course or grade that will move them toward that end? This establishes the horizontal curriculum.

The "Big Ideas" that were previously developed for the levels and/or grades can be beneficial for this process. These Big Ideas can represent the key horizontal components of the curriculum and help to guide development of what would be expected from students by the end of the year. Remember, it was from these Big Ideas and the concepts and skills related to each of them that the program standards eventually evolved.

The course standards will be similar to the program standards, but will be more general in nature. Each of the program standards should be covered by one or more course standards.

Figure 9.5.
Course Standards

in Figure 9.6. In some cases, especially in the fine arts, course standards might be the same for the entire level. This occurs for the benefit of teachers who instruct in those courses (e.g., see "Physical Education" in Figure 9.6) because they instruct multiple grades at the same time. For them, there can be one single Planned Course. Differentiation in what the students learn from year to year occurs through the lesson standards.

Unit Standards

Next, the design team members should turn their attention to "unit" standards. Figure 9.7 describes this activity. The grade or course standards are further broken down into student learning behaviors, which are more defined and measurable. The unit behaviors are designed from the skills and concepts that were identified under

Music: High School (Instrumental)

- Define the technical skills necessary to master the instrument as a means of artistic, expressive performance.
- Perform a wide variety of instrumental pieces reflecting various individuals and cultures.
- Evaluate music performances utilizing informed musical judgments.

Technology Education: Eighth Grade

- Use tools, machines, and materials to design, produce, test, and analyze a product system.
- Describe the technological processes used in manufacturing, construction, transportation, and communication.
- Explore technological systems to develop career awareness and individual interests.

Physical Education: Kindergarten to Fourth Grade

- Develop body awareness and kinesthetic sense.
- Acquire manipulative skills in sports and games.
- Perform activities promoting physical fitness.
- Demonstrate cooperation and mutual respect in group games and activities.
- Show ability and knowledge in various team sports.

Health: Fourth Grade

- Develop knowledge of injury prevention and treatment.
- Describe the components of a healthy diet.
- Practice personal hygiene and identify components of physical fitness.
- Identify the body systems and their functions.
- Identify the physical, emotional, and social needs of a healthy lifestyle.

Figure 9.6.
Sample Course Standards

each of the strand areas (see Activity 6, "Strand Extension," in Chapter 6). Staying with third grade, a few of the key skills and concepts that were identified for some of the strands are shown in Box 9.1.

Description

The grade or course standards will be broken down further into learning standards that are more measurable. These "unit standards" can be designed from the skills and concepts that were identified under each of the "Big Ideas." In addition to the Big Ideas, you may also want to analyze the benchmarks for major themes. The unit standards will begin to further define the clarity of focus that is desired for the curriculum and planned course.

The unit standards should relate to the course standards, which in turn relate to the program standards.

Figure 9.7.
Unit Standards

Box 9.1 *Sample Skills and Concepts*

Geography	*Economics*	*Political Science*	*Sociology*
Map skills	Supply and demand	Voting	Cultures
Landforms	Basic needs	Rules/laws	Institutions
Natural resource maps	Production and consumption	Structure: Local/ state/national	
Communities and regions			

A sample of unit standards developed from the above is shown in Figure 9.8. To further define the clarity of focus: The unit behaviors (the curriculum standards) that students will be taught relate to the course, which, in turn, relates to the program (the content standards).

When integration of curriculum is a desired direction for the organization, the units can also be developed around major themes that would enable integration of one or more academic areas. Themes can be fun and exciting for students, increasing their motivation to learn. Themes organize the content and create manageable chunks of connected ideas for integrated learning from several disciplines. For example, themes (National Council for Social Studies, 1994) that could emerge and relate to third grade social studies would be:

- Culture
- Power, Authority, and Governance
- Production, Distribution, and Consumption
- People, Places, and Environment

I.   GEOGRAPHY

- Explore different communities in regions of both the United States and the world.

- Use maps to identify bodies of water and continents.

- Show the relationship of landforms and natural resources to the development of communities.

- Be able to use a natural resource map.

II. ECONOMICS

- Define needs and wants.

- Define the relationship between producer/consumer and supply/demand.

- List the steps in the process of developing a natural resource into a product.

- Illustrate how goods and services are distributed.

III. GOVERNMENT

- Assess what power is, its form, and how it is used.

- Relate who has the power in the local, state, and national governments.

IV. SOCIOLOGY

- Identify institutions that play a role in people's lives.

- Describe the way institutions contribute to the community.

- Identify the way institutions impact the individual.

Figure 9.8.
Examples of Unit Standards

The standards for social studies would remain the same as previously described, while standards from other academic areas would be incorporated as they apply to the appropriate theme. For example, a theme that emerged in the fifth grade Social Studies was Time, Continuity, and Change. A topic within the theme concentrated on Native Americans. For interdisciplinary study, the topic of *Native Americans* was used by Social Studies, Music, and English staff to do an integrated unit while still addressing their own individual program standards. The standard, benchmark, and performance indicator addressed to each area can be seen in Box 9.2.

Box 9.2 *An Example of an Integrated Unit*

Social Studies

Standard: Identify and describe cultural similarities and differences.

Benchmark: Exhibit a knowledge of the culture and achievements of various groups.

Performance Indicator: Develop an awareness of the culture and influence of Native Americans.

English

Standard: Compose and make oral presentations that are designed to persuade, inform, or describe.

Benchmark: Develop organization skills in writing to compose ideas for an oral presentation.

Performance Indicator: Compose and present orally an original descriptive passage.

Music

Standard: Evaluate and respond critically to works from the visual and performing arts and literature of various individuals and cultures, showing an understanding of important features of the work.

Benchmark: Interpret music performances that reflect a wide variety of people, styles, and times.

Performance Indicator: Demonstrate and critique the music of different cultures.

Specific lesson standards would be developed for each discipline, but some basic activities would connect the areas. These might include having the students do research on Native American contributions (including music) to the white culture in social studies and then summarize the findings through t-charts or a concept web. The students could then use the chart or web in their English class to compose a paper and oral presentation describing these contributions. For music, the students could critique and then perform Native American songs.

Description

The last link in the backward-mapping process is the "lesson standards." The lesson standards should relate to the units that were developed and should also be the mechanism that enables students to attain the knowledge, skills, behaviors, attitudes, and competencies required for the performance indicators. In other words, when you look at the performance indicators required for your grade or grades, what must you teach the students through your daily lessons that will enable them to be successful when the benchmarks and performance indicators are assessed?

Look at the assessments that were developed. Now, what must you teach your students through the daily lessons that will enable them to be successful on the assessment?

The daily lesson is the most specific and the most measurable in the standard sequence. Now, the lessons lead not only to the units but also define what is required for the performance indicators and then, in turn, relate to the course, which connects to the program standards.

Figure 9.9.
Lesson Standards

Lesson Standards

Finally, daily "lesson" standards that relate to the units or themes are developed. The daily lessons are yet more measurable and are the cornerstone of the backward-mapping process. It is through these daily lessons (curriculum standards) that students will receive the knowledge and skills to perform the assessments and ultimately to demonstrate their acquired knowledge of and skill in the content standards. The description for this activity is provided in Figure 9.9.

A Lesson Guide that was developed for this purpose, along with an example of a daily lesson(s), is shown in Figure 9.10. The box labeled "Standard Link" shows how that particular lesson or series of lessons relates to the content standard. Please note the connection between the lesson (curriculum) standards shown in Figure 9.10 and the benchmarks and performance indicators for Standard II back in Figure 7.9 (see Chapter 7). The students will be able to perform the assessments described in Figures 8.5 and 8.6 (see Chapter 8) both while they are learning the skill and after they have acquired it.

There may be one or several standards on a page. The teacher may cover the standards in one class period or may take several.

Note that the reference section at the bottom of Figure 9.10 is part of the Planned Course. The reference section can be consulted by the

Grade/Subject: _____

Standard Link	
Standard Link	
Program Standard(s)	II
Benchmark(s)	II, 1-3
Performance Indicator(s)	1A, 1B, 2A, 3A

Lesson Standard(s):   **Date Completed**

The student will:

- Define, locate, and identify the seven continents and four oceans
- Explain how a community grows because of its natural resources
- Compare and contrast differences in communities

Reference Section:

Content/Skills, Methods, Materials   Page _____

Core Activities, Enrichment, Reteaching   Page _____

Figure 9.10.
Sample Lesson Guide

Program Standard	Benchmark	Performance Indicator
The student will be able to explain how geography affects the interdependency of location, place, movement, regions, and human interaction.	Identify basic topographical terms (e.g., river, mountain, ocean).	1B. Define and label landforms and bodies of water. (3)
	Compare and contrast differences in communities.	Identify urban, rural, and suburban communities. (2-3)

Course Standard:

- Illustrate and explain basic concepts of geography.

Unit/Theme Standards:

- Explore different communities in regions of the United States and the world.
- Use maps to identify bodies of water and continents.
- Show the relationship of landforms and natural resources to the development of communities.

Lesson Standards:

- Define, locate, and identify the seven continents and four oceans.
- Explain how a community grows because of its natural resources.
- Compare and contrast differences in communities.

Figure 9.11.
Backward Map

instructor for additional help on selection of materials, suggestions for instructional methods, sample activities, and enrichment and reteaching activities as they pertain to the standards addressed.

Now, the lessons lead to the units or themes that relate to the course, which ties into the program. See Figure 9.11 for an example of how one standard from the social studies program that we have identified would be addressed at each of the levels on one schematic. The backward mapping of that standard is from the top. At each lower level, the standard becomes more specific and measurable. Although the Planned Course is designed from the top down, from general to specific, the instruction begins at the bottom and works up. With each lesson or series of lessons, the *curriculum standards* are being met because the lessons relate to units/themes, course, and program. The lessons enable the students to become equipped with the knowledge and skill that will be required to demonstrate the performance indicators that define the benchmarks and ultimately the program *content standards*.

Alternative Organizer

A second type of organizer developed for the lesson standards enables the teacher to select from a series of menus at the top (see Figure 9.12) to address not only the content standard but also the life-long standards that will give the well-educated student the kinds of critical skills the organization believes are important. This "Alternative Lesson Guide" is shown in Figure 9.12. To clarify further: The lesson in this unit is geometry, and the standard for the lesson is to construct geometric figures with a compass and ruler. A traditional approach to this lesson might consist of providing some background information and then distributing the necessary equipment to the students for the activity. The lesson might end with some of the students displaying their work.

By utilizing the organizer and its menus, the teacher could intervene with some additional skills. For example, under the menu titled Life-Long Standards, a decision might be made to include an activity in communication. Written communication could be emphasized at the end of the instruction by having students write in their journals what they learned or what they felt was the hardest or easiest part of the lesson, or by having them send a letter to an absent classmate, explaining the activities for the day. Oral communication could be emphasized by having the students verbally summarize what they learned.

In the Skills menu, the teacher may decide to have the students construct their geometric figures on a computer—rather than use traditional materials—to enhance their technological capabilities. In the Connections menu, a deliberate effort might be made to show how this lesson relates to something that has been done previously or that will be coming in the future. The lesson could also be related to some other subject or life situation as a mechanism for creating meaning or relevancy for the student. Remember, cognitive research tells us that the more meaning students see in the learning, the greater their chance for retention of that information or skill in long-term memory.

Someone else may choose other ways to deliver the lesson, possibly by having the students work in groups as a way of promoting group effectiveness (see the Life-Long Standards in Figure 9.12) or by having the task involve problem solving (part of the Skills menu). On the back of the organizer, the teacher can describe the instructional strategies. The key to this process is knowing that some students will not learn the information or skills on the first pass of instruction. For second chance opportunities, rather than presenting the information in the manner that was unsuccessful the first time, the teacher can now seek out alternative methods that were used by colleagues and thereby expand his or her personal repertoire of strategies.

Life-Long Standards		Skills		Connections	
Communications	_____	Problem Solving	_____	Math Lesson	_____
Problem Solving	_____	Communication	_____	Math Unit	_____
Critical Thinking	_____	Technology	_____	Other Subjects	_____
Group Effectiveness	_____	Reasoning	_____	Life Situation	_____
Technology	_____	Estimation	_____	Learning Strategy	_____

Strand/Theme: Geometry

Lesson Standard(s):

The student will:

Construct geometric figures with a compass and ruler

Materials Needed: Text Page: _____

Figure 9.12.
Alternative Lesson Guide

Obviously, one of the keys to this scheme is the ability to incorporate life-long standards into the academic area as part of the process. Figure 9.13 shows an assessment designated as a group project and that occurred after a period of instruction in a high school science class. In this assessment, the teacher not only evaluated students' acquisition of science content, but also used the project to gather feedback on their ability to communicate through effective writing (as it pertained to a science audience) and their ability to work collaboratively in a group situation. The tools used to assess the project were holistic rubrics that can be seen in Figures 9.14, 9.15, and 9.16.

So, the teacher was not only able to assess the demonstration of knowledge and skills related to science standards but also the demonstration of life-long standards that the district believed all students should acquire in order to be prepared for the future.

Each life-long standard had operational definitions, as previously discussed. These operational definitions were incorporated into a variety of rubrics. The rubrics were distributed to all staff members through an assessment tool kit. The tool kit promoted both staff development and the expectation of providing all students with as many experiences as possible to develop the life-long standards. As the staff assessed their students on the content standards, they could use the rubrics to assess the life-long standards when that was appropriate.

The random education discussed earlier was now being replaced with a curriculum that was designed strategically and aligned with assessment practices.

Other Planned Course Elements

The flowchart and corresponding definitions shown earlier in Figures 9.3 and 9.4 identified other elements of the Planned Course. Each of these elements simply serves to enhance further the delivery of the standards. Each Planned Course contains a reference section that the teacher can consult when implementing the curriculum. This reference section identifies the content and skills that make up the content standards. It provides a list of instructional activities that might be used to help students acquire the content and skill needed to achieve the standards. There are also suggestions for instructional strategies to deliver the lessons; enrichment activities for those students who demonstrate performance of the standards after initial assessment has occurred; and reteaching activities that provide variations of activities, methods, or both, for those students who do not initially meet performance specifications.

Assessment Type: _____ **Formative** __X__ **Summative**

Academic Area(s):

Outcome Link	
Standard(s)	_____
Benchmark(s)	_____
Performance Indicator(s)	_____

Group Project:

Students will be assigned to groups and will develop a project and presentation on one of the following issues with regard to the environment:

- Deforestation
- Air Pollution
- Toxic Waste Disposal
- Solid Waste Disposal
- Thermal Pollution
- Acid Problems
- Radioactive Waste Disposal
- Global Warming
- Desertification/Soil Erosion
- Ozone Depletion
- Water Pollution

In order to have a complete presentation and group effort:

Presentation:

- Give specific examples of the problem.
- Show evidence, in forms of scientific research that was done, that the problem exists.
- Supply specific causes of the problem.
- Give a prediction of what may happen if the problem is permitted to continue.
- Provide several possible solutions to the problem.
- What is currently being done to solve the problem?
- What will this solution cost the public?
- Could the solution to this problem cause another problem?

Group Requirements:

- Each member of the group must present for at least 5 minutes.
- Transition between group members must be smooth.
- There must be a definite introduction and conclusion.
- The group must be prepared to answer questions at the end.
- Each member of the group must have a visual aid that relates to the presentation.

Methods

Teacher Observation
Student Log
Peer Observation
Student Journal
Event Task
Student Project
Observational Checklist
Peer Assessment
Interview
Role-Playing
Anecdotal Comments
Student Self-Assessment
Group Project
Student Report
Formal Task
Parental Report
Written Test
Other

Performance Standards: Rubrics are provided for content, communication skills, and collaboration skills

Figure 9.13.
Science Assessment: Content and Life-Long Standards

SCALE AND STANDARDS

Distinguished (4)	Proficient (3)	Apprentice (2)	Novice (1)	Unacceptable (0)
Demonstrates a thorough understanding by providing essential information about the environmental problem and provides new insights and/or solutions to the problem.	Displays a complete and accurate understanding of the effects of the environmental problem by providing essential information and/or a correct solution, but with an explanation that lacks clarity and/or has minor error(s).	Displays an incomplete understanding of the effects of the environmental problem due to missing information or inappropriate information, and has an incorrect solution due to minor errors or appropriate information that is implemented incorrectly.	Demonstrates severe misconceptions about the effects of the environmental problem through one or more incorrect approaches attempted or explained. Most key elements are missing.	Displays some information about the environmental problem but explanation is not provided or is completely incorrect, indecipherable, or irrelevant.

Figure 9.14.
Holistic Rubric: Science Content

SCALE AND STANDARDS

Distinguished (4)	Proficient (3)	Apprentice (2)	Novice (1)	Unacceptable (0)
Clearly and effectively communicates the main idea or theme and provides support that contains vivid detail. Presents information in a style that capitalizes on the audience's level of understanding. Creates a visual that exceeds conventional standards.	Clearly communicates the main idea or theme and provides suitable support and detail. Presents information in a style and tone consistent with the audience's level of understanding. Creates a visual that clearly meets conventional standards.	Communicates important information, but without a clear theme or overall structure. Presents information in a style or tone inappropriate to the audience's level of understanding. Creates a visual that is missing one or more key elements.	Communicates information as isolated pieces in a random fashion. Presents information in a style and tone inappropriate to the audience's level of understanding. Creates a substandard visual.	Expression of ideas, audience interest, and knowledge is missing, irrelevant, or incomplete. Visual is missing.

Dimensions & Definitions

	Ideas	Strategies	Audience
	• Able to express ideas clearly.	• Utilizes a visual	• Intended receiver of the information

Figure 9.15.
Holistic Rubric: Communication Skills

SCALE AND STANDARDS

Distinguished (4)	Proficient (3)	Apprentice (2)	Novice (1)	Unacceptable (0)
Actively helps to identify group goals and works hard to meet them.	Communicates commitment to the group goals and effectively carries out assigned roles.	Communicates commitment to the group goals, but does not carry out assigned roles.	Does not work toward group goals or actively works against them.	Group goals are completely missing, indecipherable, or irrelevant.

Dimensions & Definitions

Group Goals	Role Performance			
• The identified task	• Tasks assigned or assumed by members			

Figure 9.16.
Holistic Rubric: Collaboration Skills

Summary

The content standards defined by the benchmarks and performance indicators are translated into curriculum standards through the development of a Planned Course of Study. The Planned Course is designed through a process called backward mapping. The backward mapping process designs course, unit, and lesson curriculum standards that define the content standards. The Planned Course is additionally enhanced by related instructional activities and strategies, assessments, and suggestions for enrichment and reteaching. The result is a curriculum with a purpose—a curriculum developed with the best knowledge available related to what students need for the future. In addition, the curriculum informs students, parents, and teachers of what is expected from students after 13 years of instruction. No longer will we have to say that curriculum is taught because everybody knows that we need it or because the state requires it. Rather, we can say that the curriculum is a strategic design for our preferred vision of what students need for success in the future.

CHAPTER TEN

Attending to Other Curriculum Details

Chapters 6, 7, and 9 detailed each of the specific components essential in the design of a standards-based curriculum. Before we move ahead with the final two chapters, which deal with instruction and with leadership, I would like to discuss briefly what traditionally become the missing elements when dealing with curriculum: *Preparation, Implementation,* and *Evaluation.*

While I believe that most school systems, in general, have some system or mechanism for the design of curriculum, I also believe that organizations have a tendency not to deal with the entire scope of the curriculum development process.

Areas that seem to receive the least attention include monitoring the implementation of new curriculum, evaluating the impact of the curriculum on student achievement, and an ongoing mechanism for preparing for the review of an academic area.

Organizational leaders need to develop a comprehensive K-through-12 approach to curriculum design and implementation that enables the district staff to understand, define, and see the links among elementary, middle, and high school curriculum.

Leaders must realize the importance of these often forgotten elements and see the need to bring them into the process. We now expand the Framework for Excellence that was described in Chapter 2 by again going inside to include preparation, implementation, and evaluation. In the expanded model, shown in Figure 10.1, you now see the design components placed within the overall developmental process.

Preparation

In most organizations, preparation may include identifying a curriculum review team and scheduling team meetings on district inservice days to review the current curriculum and make recommendations for change. The review could also simply represent choosing new textbooks without engaging in any activities to determine the future academic needs of the students.

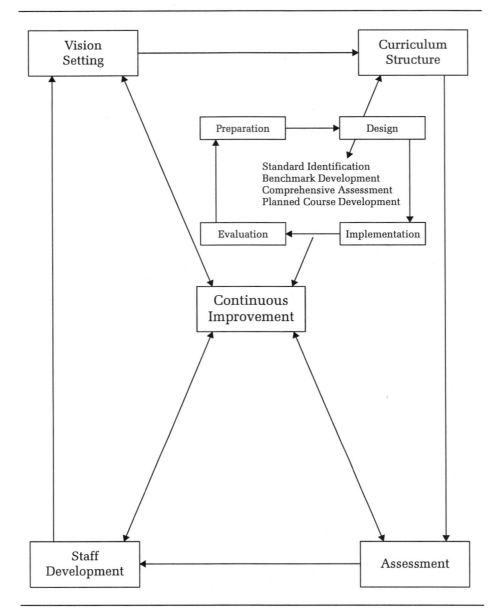

Figure 10.1.
Expanded Framework for Excellence

When preparing to develop a standards-based curriculum, it is advisable to establish a Curriculum Advisory Panel. The group should be made up of representatives from central office, building administration, and faculty that includes both regular and special education. The responsibilities of this group would include—but not be limited to—the following steps, which are necessary to produce a standards driven organization:

- Appointing curriculum development teams
- Developing the knowledge base for curriculum, instruction, assessment, and other related areas

- Orienting staff
- Collecting data
- Securing resources
- Scheduling meetings
- Managing all the key details that are required before, during, and after the curriculum development process

Implementation

After the curriculum has been designed it is all too often neglected, if not forgotten, during the implementation process. The district leaders responsible for the design of the curriculum are soon off to the next academic area or project and the new curriculum being implemented becomes a check mark on a task list.

Implementation may be the most important element in the process, because it defines the time when the new standards-based curriculum will be utilized. As mentioned earlier in the book, implementation of a curriculum or a program can result in random education for the students when staff are not a part of the vision-setting or planning process, do not see the need for change, or do not possess the skills to make a vision become reality.

When implementing a standards-based curriculum it is therefore imperative that staff have an opportunity to discuss the strengths and weaknesses of the curriculum on an ongoing basis. This can be accomplished through ongoing assessment that documents both the successes and problems of implementing the curriculum along with the results of student performance. Some tools utilized in this procedure will be discussed below.

In our schools, our vision for preparing students for the future was a collaborative process undertaken by many different stakeholders from within and outside the organization. Staff development gave all staff the necessary skills to realize the intended vision. Once they were trained, the staff had high expectations of implementing the desired future in a planned, organized, and systematic way.

In addition, we have found implementation is more successful when it follows a prescribed sequence of *Readiness, Pre-Implementation, Implementation,* and *Community Involvement.*

In the Readiness cycle, a phase-in process is used for the development of standards and planned courses. In other words, we limit our activities to one or two academic areas in a given year. Even though the vision setting (the strategic planning discussed earlier) has allowed us to develop the big picture, we start small so that staff are not overwhelmed with too much change at any one time.

In the Pre-Implementation cycle, teams of teachers review the best knowledge available with regard to major national curriculum projects, the recommendations of experts, and effective teaching and learning in that field. The teams may also visit exemplary programs as they prepare. This part of the cycle allows the staff to begin reviewing the literature to see what is suggested as a direction for the future. In other words, prior to beginning their academic review, they have an opportunity to spend time analyzing futuristic thinking and discussing potential impacts upon their curriculum. This allows comparisons with the current status of the program and, most important, increases the knowledge base of the staff. All too often curriculum revision results in duplicating the old way under a few different names, unless the staff has the opportunity to see, discuss, and evaluate new trends and ideas. So, when the team eventually meets to design and discuss an exemplary program, the members can utilize information that represents a combination of their craft experience and recommendations from the field. The combination enables the team to produce a revised curriculum that truly represents the needs for the future.

During Implementation, there should be a comprehensive training plan for the staff. This plan should include the training of key staff members to lead the design process, presentation of the new curriculum to all staff, regular follow-up meetings for sharing and revising the curriculum, and resource people to serve as counsel when problems arise with the implementation.

Last, the Community Involvement cycle provides the opportunity for residents not only to be aware of new curriculum revisions and proposals but also to communicate their areas of concern. The advantage of this aspect is that it negates (to some degree) the surprise element of change efforts going to the public and concerns coming back to the organization.

Evaluation and Continuous Improvement

Evaluation of the overall curriculum and specific Planned Courses should be an ongoing process. As the implementation process begins, regular meetings should be held to discuss the effectiveness of the curriculum being delivered. This enables the staff to deal with concerns, discuss issues as they arise, and feel that support is always available.

Your system should have some type of evaluation tool to direct the process; an example of one type is provided in Figures 10.2 and 10.3. As you review the instruments in these figures, you will see that they align with the construction of the Planned Course that was discussed in Chapter 9. Through the use of the tools, data are collected that will enable decision makers to make informed recommendations on the need for further refinements or changes to the curriculum. This

---

Directions

Use the *analytic rubric* attached to respond to the questions below. If your response to any of the questions is less than *Exemplary*, please indicate what action is needed to move to *Exemplary*.

1. The time frame suggested for implementing themes, units, or lessons was appropriate.

2. The available materials, resources, and technology were adequately used.

3. The instructional methods were effective.

4. The relevance of the content and skills was clear to the students.

5. There was communication with colleagues relative to the curriculum.

6. Assessment indicates students are successfully achieving the curriculum.

7. Students were given appropriate enrichment/relearning activities.

Comments:

Question:

What changes must be made to improve any aspect of this curriculum as it relates to: lesson, unit, course (curriculum standards), and the content standards as defined by the benchmarks and performance indicators?

Figure 10.2.
Evaluation Tool

mechanism not only identifies problems but also ensures that steps are taken to use the data in a way that initiates improvement action for better teacher and student performance on a continuous basis.

This process sends a very powerful message to staff and community that continuous improvement is a cornerstone belief and will serve as a main cog in operating the schools to meet the needs of students.

Summary

The curriculum process represents more than just design. For it to be truly comprehensive, it is important that any organization engaging in an ongoing process of curriculum development incorporate Preparation, Implementation, and Evaluation.

PLANNED COURSE EVALUATION

Elements	Exemplary	Developing	Beginning
Time Frame	The time appropriated for delivering the content and skills defined in the Planned Course follows the developmental needs of the students.	Meets the developmental needs of the students in some areas but not all.	Does not match the developmental needs of the students in any area.
Materials/Resources & Technology	Variety of materials/resources and technology are available, relevant, and widely used for the course and student use.	Some materials/resources and technology are available for use. Available items are relevant to the curriculum being delivered.	Limited materials/resources and technology available. Those that are available have little relevance to the curriculum being delivered.
Instructional Methods	Varied and represent the best available to deliver the standards. Practices reflect various learner styles.	Have a relationship to the standards. Practices are a combination of traditional lecture and class participation with teacher-facilitated experiences.	Based on content and show little relationship to achieving the standards. Practices are teacher-led and traditional in their design.
Curriculum Relevance	Students view the curriculum as meaningful and are motivated to engage in learning activities on a regular basis.	Students view parts of the curriculum as meaningful and then exhibit motivation to learn.	Students see no relevance in any aspect of the written and delivered curriculum.
Colleague Communication	Meetings within grade levels, departments, teams are held on a regular basis to discuss the implementation process. Discussion provides a basis for identifying strengths and weaknesses.	Meetings held randomly within grade levels, departments, teams to discuss implementation.	Meetings rarely held. When they do occur, the discussion is not relevant to the curriculum and its implementation. Discussion is somewhat productive in highlighting strengths and/or issues of concern.
Student Achievement	Students perform to high skill expectation. Students take responsibility for the learning and see it as beneficial and relevant.	Students perform to above average skill expectations. The teacher maintains responsibility for most learning. Students cannot identify the benefit or relevancy of learning.	Student performance has not changed. The teacher maintains responsibility for all learning. Students are unmotivated.
Enrichment/ Relearning	The variety of enrichment/ relearning activities enabled me to provide the needed experiences necessary for the students.	Materials were available for enrichment/relearning activities but I was not able to provide activities on a regular basis due to other factors.	Materials were not available, but even if they were, I would not provide these activities.

Figure 10.3.
Analytic Rubric

CHAPTER ELEVEN

Aligning Instruction

In his book *Developing the Curriculum*, Oliva (1982) asks the following question: "How does a teacher decide which instructional strategies to use?" He also suggests that if the teacher is lucky, he or she may be fortunate enough to find a curriculum guide that will detail not only strategies to use but also objectives, suggested resources, and suggested evaluation techniques. As you have seen, the design process and resulting Planned Course described in *Restructuring Around Standards* identifies each of those components.

The curriculum design decisions have now been made. The standards are established, and the backward mapping process has embedded them at the classroom level. The next step is the connection between the curriculum and instruction.

Although the design of the curriculum has engaged decision makers in a programmatic task, the tie to instruction revolves around tools or strategies related to methodology. These tools or strategies are determined during two phases of instruction—planning and operation.

The Planning Phase

In the planning phase, the critical question is: What strategies are best for directing the learning? The planning phase includes identification of content standards and specification of curriculum standards. Each are ultimately defined by the lesson standards at the classroom level, which are contained in the Planned Course.

For instance, Figure 11.1 is similar to the backward map shown earlier in Chapter 9. The example in Figure 11.1 is from fifth grade social studies. A content standard is shown in the top box and defined by the benchmark and performance indicator, followed by the curriculum standards addressed in the Planned Course. In this case, the theme is Time, Continuity, and Change. While there are other content standards addressed in this theme, the example shows only the piece that relates to that portion of the theme. Each of the lesson standards will be implemented through a choice of instructional tools or strategies.

Content Standard	Benchmark	Performance Indicator
The student will be able to demonstrate an understanding of people, places, and events throughout U.S. and world history.	Demonstrate knowledge of historical development of Pennsylvania and the United States.	Identify various Indian groups.

Course Standards

- Develop an awareness of the cultures of Native Americans and of Native Americans' relationships to European settlers.
- Describe how individuals, institutions, or groups affected change in American history up to 1850.
- Incorporate historical information into age-appropriate projects.
- Use critical thinking to analyze problems and solutions that developed in early U.S. history.

Theme: Time, Continuity, and Change

- Explain how and why people first came to America.
- Discuss how and why the various Native American cultures developed.
- Identify similarities and differences among the various Native American groups.

Lesson Standards

- Identify the first America and explain why they migrated to North America.
- Identify the location of traditional Indian cultures of North America on a map.

Figure 11.1.
Backward Map

With the Planned Course identifying the academic areas to be addressed through the implementation of the standards, the classroom teacher is now ready to identify the appropriate instructional strategies to deliver the standards through the planning phase.

The teacher may ask these questions:

- What is the best way to go about teaching this lesson, topic, or theme?
- What methods shall I use?
- What strategies are appropriate?
- What do I know about my students and their learning styles?

For the example shown in Figure 11.1, a corresponding assessment might ask the students to work in cooperative groups to create a chart of various Indian groups. The chart would include information, descriptions, or both, about environment, clothing, shelter, food, and other related items.

The Operational Phase

In the operational phase, the teacher implements the strategies and evaluates the instruction. The teacher determines the appropriate strategy for delivering the standards by choosing a method for delivering the curriculum. A strategy ordinarily includes multiple procedures or techniques.

For example, a popular method and the one all of us have used the most is lecturing. While the strategy is the lecture, the procedure during the lecture might call for handing out charts and conducting a formative assessment at the conclusion of the lesson, perhaps a journal entry identifying questions encountered or future application of the content or skills learned. Another technique that may be used during the lecture might be checking for understanding, which would be a generic teaching skill.

Some of the more common instructional strategies include lecture, small group discussion, deduction, induction, questioning, problem solving, programmed instruction, discovery or inquiry, tutoring, cooperative learning, repetitive drill, independent study, and so on.

Teachers generally tend to choose strategies at random or strategies that fall within their preferred teaching style. It is important to align instructional strategies with the curriculum and assessment.

We now know what we want the student to know and be able to do. We know how the curriculum will be assessed. *So, if we know what we want the students to know and/or be able to do, and we know the method(s) for assessing that knowledge or skill, the next key ingredient of alignment is to determine the best way to teach (instruct) the students in what they need to know or be able to do in order to be successful on the assessment.*

Selecting Strategies

When aligning the strategy with the curriculum and the assessment, the teacher has traditionally had several sources to consult. The broadest source is often defined by the subject matter itself. Looking at the subject matter, the teacher would ask what concepts, skills, behaviors, and the like, must be learned by the student.

In the curriculum development process we have just reviewed, the knowledge and skills to be obtained by the students have been specifically identified for the teacher. The strategies should now be used to attempt to engage the learners in the instructional process, to place them in real situations with relevant and meaningful context or even in a simulated environment.

In general, the teacher should look at the subject area standards, the performance indicators, and the intended method of assessment and ask how he or she can engage the students in instructional practices that are meaningful and relevant. Teachers must also remember to examine the specific classroom lesson standards. Once again, these are the key links that will provide the students with the knowledge and skills to demonstrate the content standards.

While these might appear to present an unlimited number of strategies, the ones that are appropriate to the content and skill to be acquired in a particular lesson or series of lessons will be limited. Returning to the example given in Figure 11.1: Since the assessment could involve a cooperative group activity, it would probably be wise to have the students acquire the needed information through cooperative learning.

As a second example, recall the lesson standard discussed in Chapter 9 (see Figure 9.12) that asked the students to construct geometric figures with a compass and ruler. Possible strategies for delivering this lesson might include:

- Telling the students how to perform the task
- Repetition with several examples
- Chalk talk and demonstration
- Workbook practice
- Computer simulation
- Laser disk examples

When identifying the possible strategies, it is also important to remember that not all strategies will be appropriate to the teacher's instructional style or to the students' learning style. The range of possibilities is thus limited.

For the lesson above, since acquisition of technological skills is an important life-long standard, the teacher may choose to utilize the computer simulation for the strategy to deliver that particular curriculum standard.

For a third example, let's use a previously identified content standard: *Use the writing process to compose texts*. In order to demonstrate this standard, the teacher would need to engage the students in a number of lesson standards that could focus on the acquisition of such skills as prewriting, drafting, revising through both self- and peer evaluation, editing, and publishing. The assessment could be a process portfolio that represents the five skills just mentioned. Instructional strategies that would match the delivery of those skills could include the following:

- Prewriting activities
- Modeling
- Self-selection of writing topics
- Mini lessons
- Teacher conference
- Peer evaluation and conferencing
- Peer editing
- Self-evaluation

In other cases the strategy may be obvious—the standard is the strategy:

- Write an editorial
- Demonstrate the high jump
- Sew a zipper into a garment

Also remember that some subject areas are naturally more difficult than others—calculus, chemistry, and the like. In these cases, the strategies may be very straightforward: lecture and demonstration followed by practice and assessment.

Lastly, when making final selections for strategies, be sure that the strategies are appropriate for the students, relevant, and developmentally appropriate. The strategies should match the teacher's personal style of teaching. It is important that teachers analyze their own particular style of teaching and determine preferences and the styles that would be complementary. For example, choosing large group instruction as a strategy would not appeal to someone who prefers to work closely with students. At the same time, it is also critical to ensure that personal needs do not limit what the students receive. Be careful not to choose only methods that match individual style when a particular strategy would be appropriate for the intended learning and assessment.

Evaluating Instruction

After the curriculum has been delivered through the chosen strategies, it is vital to assess not only the students' achievement, but also the teacher's performance and the effectiveness of the instructional strategy.

When students do poorly, it is very easy to assume or convince ourselves that they did not pay attention, did not study, or were careless in their responses. However, it would be much more appropriate to self-assess individual performance and the design of the curriculum.

Remember the discussion in Chapter 10 about the importance of including comprehensive staff training, follow-up meetings for sharing curriculum-related concerns, and using tools to collect data on student performance that will enable decision makers to determine the appropriateness of the curriculum. We should therefore use a variety of ways to determine if the standards were appropriate and relevant to the students. It is to be hoped that the design process addressed this, but only implementation will tell the true story. A curriculum generally looks good on paper; it isn't until implementation that we know for sure if the students possessed the entry level skills to be successful or if the strategies chosen to match the assessment and deliver the standards complemented the learning styles of the students.

Another important question should be: Did the pupils have sufficient time to respond? A response from a sixth-grade student to a math assessment is quoted below:

> I thought that the baseball test was hard. You said if you don't finish they will be wrong. So I rushed through them to see if I could get any points. I did not. I think if I could have taken my time, as long as I needed I could get a better grade. I got an E, I do not feel good. If I could take it over, I could do better.

Continuous improvement for any organization occurs when that organization is committed to implementing a process of collecting information that will assess the decisions made when designing their learning system.

Summary

Begin with the learners and choose strategies that meet their needs and interests and that are relevant, developmentally appropriate, and match their learning style. Look at the content standard as defined by the benchmarks and performance indicators. What are you looking for and how are you going to assess it? What strategies are available for daily lessons; will they deliver the curriculum standards? Also ask if the strategy will work for you and whether the subject matter itself defines the strategy. Lastly, from a practical standpoint, determine the amount of time available. If a strategy will take several days and there is a limited amount of time, it may not be feasible to implement. Some strategies may also require more resources than are available or accessible. Most important, will the selected strategies provide the students with the knowledge and skill to demonstrate the chosen assessment?

CHAPTER TWELVE

Leading a Standards-Based Organization

The history of American education is, in large part, the history of recurring cycles of reform. There is considerable disagreement over the meaning and effects of these cycles. Reform has historically had little effect on teaching and learning in the classrooms.

One of the underlying reasons change efforts fall short is that many innovations really have little to do with students and teachers in the classrooms. Instead, much of the emphasis has been on the modification of such things as organizational and administrative structures, physical plants, and academic and vocational curriculum splits.

Clearly there are many efforts to improve the quality of education, but are the changes they involve meaningful? Improvement efforts may be necessary, but they are not sufficient to bring about meaningful change. Schools can improve if they gear up to get better results by examining and refining processes that contribute to *designated or desired results*. For us, these were the results identified in the development of our strategic plan.

Attention to standards and appropriate measures of their attainment are key factors to improved performance. The cornerstone of our focus on results consists of visionary leadership; meaningful teamwork; support; and clear, measurable goals monitored through the regular collection and analysis of performance data.

Visionary Leadership

Leadership begins with vision. The critical difference between successful, dynamic leaders and others who simply occupy a leading position is a compelling sense of vision and a matching dedication to make that vision a reality (Champlin, 1990). Some leaders simply occupy a leadership position. They maintain the status quo and hope not to cause issues to surface.

In simple terms, vision is the act or power of seeing. Our challenge is to prize vision and to have all members of the organization accept that vision is encouraged and rewarded. Without vision development and renewal, organizations will have difficulty attaining a status of effectiveness.

Our profession and our organizations would be greatly enhanced if we gave the highest priority to our vision (Champlin, 1990). We have used this approach to open the door to more extensive and effective use of the professional literature. It has helped us to establish optimums, the very thing of which vision is made. Access to the literature has created the possibility for all to become visionary. Past developments in the field have produced sophisticated and critical understandings of cognition—how students learn. We have a current technology that makes it possible for practically all students to become sustained, successful learners. We have just spent significant time discussing and developing knowledge of the variables (curriculum, assessment, instruction) that must be altered and manipulated. A sense of the possible and the attainable is what differentiates vision from fantasy. Staying close to our professional data, always searching and probing, and always challenging individuals to respond by reaching for the optimum is the basis from which visions emerge.

Meaningful Teamwork

As leaders, we must always understand that vision is made into reality through people. If the vision for an organization is to become a reality, all organization members must share in it. Generating a vision is meaningless unless there is an equal ability to inspire and influence others to meet the challenges that the vision may bring (Champlin, 1990).

It is also important to remember that vision must have the power to create an image that is in some way better than the old one and to encourage others to share that aspiration. As leaders, we must see not only the picture of what might be, but also possess a well-defined view of how individuals must be trained, supported, and reinforced to be able to break successfully away from maintaining the status quo of organizational life. As leaders, we must also intentionally work to develop an organizational culture in which creative application and problem solving replace rote maintenance of the status quo. In your organization, members should be encouraged to solve complex problems even when there is uncertainty and stress. Everyone should be viewed as capable of creative behavior.

For meaningful teamwork to occur, each of us must have a sense of commitment that pervades every aspect of our behavior. Individuals in the organization must be able to identify with the beliefs that serve as guides to preferred actions and preferred personal or social forms of conduct. These are the things for which the team as a whole and its individual members will make sacrifices. Commitment to a vision means focusing on the vision, the optimum, in all organizational and individual behavior (Champlin, 1990). Our organization made a commitment to organize learning and to target professional behavior to be consistent with what the prevailing literature revealed about each. The literature related the need to foster ownership for organizational growth to occur and the need to be data driven.

Vision is crafted from research and professional literature. Vision is made attainable through effective development of the actors in the organization who buy into and gradually accept ownership. Vision can become compelling for those who understand that vision is not the right of just a few, but rather openly accessible to all.

Support

Vision in its early stages of development is often weak and thus requires special support. There are a few leader actions that can make a difference in the acceptance or rejection of a vision. Personal courage is one (Champlin, 1990). Supporting a vision that differs from the existing state of the organization is a major risk. The courage to stick by one's dedication and commitment is essential.

Resistance is a natural condition of life in an organization and for its members. New approaches and different ways of thinking can be perceived as a loss of control or as a concern for more work. Change can also bring with it excess uncertainty, the memory of past resentments, and concerns about future competence. Leaders must always remember that the natural tendency is for organizational culture to dismiss approaches that will change the status quo. There is little tolerance in organizations for actions that do change the status quo. The courage to advocate and champion change is critical.

Close on the heels of courage is perseverance. As a leader, you must have the tenacity to maintain your personal commitment and conviction while at the same time understanding that each person has his or her own tolerance level and tempo for behavioral and attitudinal adjustments (Champlin, 1990). Perseverance is not simply outwaiting adversaries; it means having a pro-active plan that keeps the vision in focus through ongoing training and dialogue. Influence from key players is constantly exerted in the hope that the ultimate end will be goals that become unmistakable.

Throughout this entire process, we must also remember that there is rarely only one way to accomplish change. Just as we now often encourage our students to seek alternative ways to solve problems, so should we be willing to seek an alternative "best way" to achieve a larger purpose. I have often found it extremely difficult, and most times not at all desirable, to specify exactly how something should be done. A staff requires some latitude in determining the most desired alternatives. A leader's vision should have firm boundaries but flexible approaches to making the vision a reality.

Finally, vision needs to have the capacity to be renewed and redefined in the light of new insights and more viable alternatives. The need for continuous improvement has been referred to throughout the book. As long as the integrity of the initial purpose is preserved, it is healthy, essential, and a normal aspect of visionary activity for alternatives to be generated. Renewal stimulates creativity and builds the opportunity for ownership and influence.

Goals and Performance Data

We have found that the success of implementing any vision or goal associated with that vision depends on establishing effective ways of getting information about how well or poorly change is going in the school or classroom. Consequently, we continually ask ourselves: What do we want for our students, and how do we know if we are getting it?

In order to answer our question, we ask staff to establish collective goals related to our vision, track them using data, and use the data to assess or adjust efforts toward better results.

In Chapter 2, several standards (part of a vision for students to possess communication skills) regarding students becoming exemplary writers were discussed. Our English department, focusing on written communication and the standards discussed in Chapter 2, established the goal of all students becoming effective writers.

With the goal established, the team members determined the performance standards that would be acceptable as effective writing and incorporated them into a predetermined rubric. Based on the rubric (see Figure 12.1, first presented as Figure 3.3), the team decided students would need to demonstrate writing skills that reached performance standard levels of *Distinguished* or *Proficient* to be considered effective writers.

The group believed that the process would be facilitated and that the students would perform better if the students were provided with the criteria (identified in the rubric) expected of them and if they could see models or "anchor papers" that specified expectations.

For this to occur, it was decided to select students randomly to write to a prompt and then assess the papers according to the rubric

Distinguished (4)	Proficient (3)	Apprentice (2)	Novice (1)	Unacceptable (0)
The focus is sharp and distinct. The content is not only substantial and specific but also illustrative with sophisticated ideas that are well developed. The structure is obviously controlled and the writer's voice is very apparent in tone, sentence structure and word choice. There are few mechanical and usage errors.	The focus is clear. The content is specific and illustrative. There is evidence of logical and appropriate structure as well as precision and variety in sentence structure and word choice. There are some mechanical and usage errors.	The focus is adequate. There is sufficient content. The structure is appropriate with some precision and variety in sentence structure and word choice. The mechanical and usage errors are not severe enough to interfere significantly with the writer's purpose.	The focus is vague. The content is limited to a listing, repetition, or mere sequence of ideas. The structure is inconsistent with limited sentence variety and word choice. There is evidence of repeated weaknesses in mechanics and usage.	The focus is very confused or absent. The content is superficial or absent of relevance. The structure is confused and there is no apparent control over sentence structure and word choice. The mechanical and usage errors severely interfere with the writer's purpose and make it nearly impossible to understand.

Dimensions

Focus	Content	Structure	Style	Mechanics
• Communicates with appropriate audience • Maintains clear focus throughout the work • Ideas are clear • Evidence of comprehension and application of knowledge	• Information organized and stated clearly • Information is complete and relevant • Ideas are concise and well developed • Supporting details are provided	• Flow is sequential • Paragraphs deal with a specific focus • All paragraphs are related, complete, and organized • Good transitions • Beginning and end are clear and effective	• Language is clear • Word choice is appropriate • Original and creative • Sentences are varied • Writing sounds natural and fluent	• Required spelling, capitalization, and punctuation • Correct and appropriate usage • Complete sentences • Paragraphing is appropriate

Figure 12.1.
Holistic Rubric

to establish examples or anchors for the students. The prompt that was given in Chapter 3 is repeated below:

> We all have a place that we would consider to be our favorite place. Think about a place that you feel has a special meaning to you. Try to remember everything that you can about this place and why it is so important to you.
>
> Through your writing, create the place as you remember it. Be sure to include enough details so that your reader can share

in the importance or significance of this place. Show why this place stands out for you.

As you write and rewrite your paper remember to

- Describe the place in detail
- Express why this place is so special to you
- Present your ideas clearly and logically
- Use words and well-constructed sentences effectively
- Check for errors and grammar usage

A team of staff used the results from this writing prompt to establish anchor papers for students in Grades 10 through 12. The anchor papers represented work that exemplified each point on the scale of the rubric (Distinguished, Proficient, Apprentice, Novice, and Unacceptable). In other words, these anchor papers could be used as guides by staff when assessing work, and they could be used by students and parents to demonstrate what work looked like in each of the categories. Students were provided with both the rubric identifying the criteria and the anchor papers that showed what examples of each criterion looked like in actual practice.

Anchor papers were also established for students in Grades K-2, 3-5, and 6-9. The results for Grades 10-12 are shown in Figures 12.2a and 12.2b.

For this exercise, the students were given standardized conditions to perform the task. The first day consisted of brainstorming and prewriting in a specified time period, and the second day of editing and making a final copy within the same time frame. Students also had the opportunity to make their work more authentic in other situations by choosing their own topics and working at their own desired pace.

The rubric provides the criteria for effective writing. The anchor papers provide examples of actual student work representing the range from Distinguished to Unacceptable. As students write and their work is assessed according to the rubric and the anchor papers, the staff analyze the results and—more important—search for clues that will indicate strengths and weaknesses in the writing. Some key questions that staff might ask themselves (Schmoker, 1996) are listed below:

- What do the data tell us? What problems or challenges do the data reveal?
- What can we do about what the data reveal? What strategies can we brainstorm?
- What do the data tell us about how effective our current efforts are in reaching the goal of all students becoming effective writers?

Unacceptable (0)	Novice (1)	Apprentice (2)
My favorite Place is a camp By house which is called Buckhill. My camp has lots of glasses and mugs, Beer Pitchers and other utensuls. My camp is on one of The highest hills around and has a Beautiful view all around. I like my camp Because is PeaceFull and away from civilization. We have Parties at my camp and also hunt there. It has two stories and is 12FT wide and 24Ft long. I like my camp Because its aplace where I can get away from People.	I would have to say that my Grandmothers house is one of my favorite places that I have. As you walk up the long and cold stair way you know when you open the door way that that room will be warm and full of love. Evert time that I go there I know that I will be surrounded by family members who care about me. When you open the door you can see the kitched which is lit by a froressent ligh Which makes everything dull. The kitchen is cenected to the spare room which I've stayed in numerous times If you backtrack you will end up in the bathroom which is small but oerfect for one person. Everything in the bathroom is neatly fixed. The towels are almost perfect after I get to them even her shampoo is set perfect. The sink is so clean that there is no visible dirt like a brand new one. You walk out of her bathroom you turn left and you will be in the living room which is emakulate There is a pile of books that is so strait it looks as if they are just a decoration. There is not one speck of dust anywhere to be found she must dust every five hours a day. Even her glasses are set perfect on the table. When you leave the living room and jaunt down the hallway the first room you will come to is her room which looks like its out of a movie not one thing out of place. I've only seen her in her room like five times and everytime it was because of me needing money. Which she has alot of but still uses coupons. her bed looks like she was in the army for about 10 years I always liked sitting on it because she got so mad. Because she always has to make it over and it takes so long. Everything is so perfect but is why it is my favorite place.	There is this special place I and several of friends of mine enjoy. This place is Seven Springs Ski Resort. We all pack into a car or truck and heatd to seven springs. we all talked and tell stories about our adventures we shared. As we go I notice the beauty of the snow on the trees, I'm not sure if my friends had noticed or not. But when we get there we unpack out of the car and head to the lodge. The lodge is huge and everything is wood and stone, amazing architecture that place is. But the place is usually packed full of people. We all get our lift tickets, food, and we sit down and discuss our plans and eat. Then we go outside to the slope and step into our skis. We ski all night, four o'clock to eleven o'clock. We all are tired and ready to hit the hay, But we head home after a night of wonderful skiing. Our trip home is quiet and Peaceful. I sometimes sleep or stare out the window and listen to the radio. We drop every body and go home. This is my favorite place to be, because I have so much fun that I will never forget as long as I live.

Figure 12.2a.
Anchor Papers

Proficient (3)	*Distinguished (4)*
A place that I will always remember is my grandfathers house. It has become a part of me and I a part of it. As I walk into each room I am hit with memories, both good and bad, which linger like ghosts refusing to leave. The house is deserted now, but nothing has been touched. It stands as the catalyst to some of the best years of my life.	A favorite place of mine my entire life has been a small cabin my father owns. I go there with my dad a couple times a year and I always enjoy myself.
The house is a small one. Its modest features probably built sometime in the twenties, paid for by the long sweaty hours my grandfather worked in a steel mill. The first thing you notice when you approach the front door is the long cracked sidewalk beneath your feet. When you open the front door immediately before you is the staircase. It is long and steep and struck fear into the hearts of many grandchildren. To your left is the living room and to your right is the kitchen and dining room.	To get to the cabin you have to follow a winding dirt road into the dense, green forest. The cabin itself is a small, cozy building made out of red brick. Inside the cabin there are two small rooms separated by a doorway with an old, dusty curtain hanging in it. One room is a small bedroom which has four bunkbeds cramped into the available space. The other room is a kitchen/living room which has a stove, an old, dirty refrigerator, a run-down couch, and old, oak table among other furnishings. The area surrounding the cabin is a very natural environment. You can see purple and green mountains on every side, and a trout-filled stream flows through the valley located just behind the cabin. There is a large, open yard filled with lush, green grass on one side of the cabin, and there is an old, rusty hand pump used to draw water up from the well located under a small apple tree. My dad's camp has always struck me as a very beautiful place.
The living room is where I spend the majority of my hours in the house. Most of my experiences consist of family gatherings or lazy Sunday afternoons. In fact, sleeping is what I did the majority of the time I was there. I used to kick one of the cousins off and have the whole couch to myself. Staying awake was a problem after about fifteen minutes. The noise of the Steeler game kind of lulled me to sleep. One of my pap's dogs would come and join me and we would snooze for hours. Our contentment would be interupted when we were gently awakened so that we could come to dinner. From the couch I would make the short walk to the cramped kitchen and sit down to eat.	I have fond memories of the time me and my dad spent at the cabin together. We would go up almost every year for the first day of fishing season. I can still remember clearly the time when I caught my first fish in a small stream near the cabin.
Dinner at grandpa's house was always special. It always consisted of pork roast and potatoes. In fact I think I ate that meal every Sunday for the first ten years of my life. I felt a happiness that cannot be explained when I was at dinner there. A kind of sense that this would not last forever and it was to be cherished. Of course nothing can last forever. Eventually family members and my grandpa died. However my memories will always live in my heart of my favorite place to be.	"Dad, I've got one!" I yelled as I felt a strong tug on my fishing pole. "Bring the net over, hurry!" As my dad approached where I was fishing, the fish stopped fighting and I thought I was snagged on some roots in the water. As my dad was about to try to unhook my line, the fish started fighting again. I eventually brought in a nice-sized rainbow trout, and it was a big thrill for me. Other fond memories include numerous hunting trips, baseball games in the yard outside, and small-stakes poker games at night.
	Even today I still have very strong feelings as far as my dad's camp goes. I always enjoyed myself immensely despite the sub-par living conditions, and I always felt these trips brought me and my dad a little closer.

Figure 12.2b.
Anchor Papers (continued)

Utilizing information generated from these questions, staff will then meet periodically to identify and track key difficulties students are having and then generate and share new interventions and materials to help students move toward their goal of becoming better writers.

While implementing any new vision or related goal, what we attempt to do (and you need to do) is to pay attention to staff issues—everything related to actual use of the new practice, such as ongoing training, staff development, time to practice, and availability of resources.

Sustained attention to continuation activities that make the vision an ongoing part of the system is critical to reaching your goals. We have found that the more time and attention devoted to the implementation phase, the more likely the program will be fully implemented. Without a doubt, the key is ongoing attention to staff concerns and meeting their needs for ongoing support and training.

Summary

We stand at the threshold of change. The biggest key to any change that may occur in your system lies with each and every individual within your organization. Each of us who are leaders in our organizations, whether we are superintendents, principals, or teachers, will set the tone for any impending change. If we are going to be successful in our efforts to create better schools or to improve upon that which we currently have, then each of us must demonstrate a leadership that will create the conditions necessary for success in our schools.

Vision has a high probability of becoming reality if leaders work systematically to develop teams, create supportive organizational capability, and be data driven. The following conditions are nurtured by leaders and are essential for organizations committed to continuous improvement. Leaders constantly strive to create organizations in which

- openness to new ideas and altered beliefs is prized and rewarded

- openness to risk-taking behavior is encouraged

- differences are tolerated and even encouraged as long as these different modes contribute to the achievement of team, department, school, organization, or system goals

- a holistic view is constantly maintained and never compromised by fragmented activities

- teamwork is prized and collaboration nurtured

- ownership for the organization's mission and purpose is essential

- expertise rather than position becomes the critical determinant in influence

Each of the above conditions contributes to the creation of an organization capable of accepting the challenge of embracing a vision and internalizing the conditions that will make it a reality. An organization is capable of producing excellence when it welcomes the challenge of reaching beyond its present state to develop new capacities. This condition is never automatic nor can it be legislated. It is, rather, the product of constant encouragement and intervention.

According to Champlin (1990), leaders are not merely visionary; they must play other roles concurrently. Leaders serve as stabilizers, carefully searching for the critical balance between maintaining the organization and stimulating new capacities. Leaders are both coaches and advisors, constantly encouraging key personnel through counsel and praise and by enabling correctives to occur as needed. Leaders facilitate and help by always taking advantage of opportunities to move progress and growth to new levels. Leaders are also visible, which allows them to model the qualities and attitudes they want to develop in others.

The leader who is an effective visionary is a person of multiple capacities. Experience has told us that vision is more likely to have impact in an organization in which the leader is viewed as much more than a dreamer, but is seen as a doer.

The critical behaviors of an effective leader can be acquired. Similarly, an individual can acquire the necessary essentials to become a visionary leader, given the willingness to address the critical issues and to demonstrate the behaviors previously described. This is not a simplistic recipe but rather a sense of the appropriate and the timely. An organization that empowers each participant with the opportunity for influence, not only in daily actions but also in envisioning and shaping the future, will have potential beyond imagining. This is a vision that is attainable.

If we are to create organizations that continuously improve, then it is imperative that leaders be equipped with the skills needed to demonstrate the essence of leadership. As you finish this book, I would ask that you evaluate your personal characteristics:

- Do I have a compelling sense of vision and a matching dedication to make a vision a reality?
- Am I a visionary who is data driven, knowledgeable about what might be, and compelled to influence others toward that state?
- Do I use my staff and colleagues to make the vision a reality?
- Do I have an articulate sense of commitment, and will I make sacrifices in order to obtain it?
- Do I have the courage to advocate a vision that differs from the existing state and possibly to risk rejection and ridicule?

Remember, vision is within the grasp of all. The issue is not who is capable of creating a vision. The challenge is to create a vision that is valued by the organization and supported by all members so that no one is afraid of what lies ahead and problems become only challenges to be met.

References

Ahlgren, A. (1993). Creating benchmarks for science education. *Educational Leadership, 5*, 46-49.

Champlin, J. R. (1990, April). *Visionary leadership.* Workshop presented at Keystone Oaks School District, Doormont, PA.

Eisner, E. W. (1995). Standards for American schools: Help or hindrance? *Phi Beta Kappan, 10*, 758-764.

Foriska, T. J. (1997). *A toolkit for developing curriculum and assessment: A facilitator's guide.* North Mankato, MN: Ten Sigma.

Glatthorn, A. (Ed.). (1995). *Content of the curriculum* (2nd ed.). Alexandria, VA: ASCD.

Larter, S., & Donnelly, J. (1993). Toronto's benchmark program. *Educational Leadership, 5*, 59-62.

Marzano, R. J., Pickering, D., & McTighe, J. (1993). *Assessing student outcomes: Performance assessment using the dimensions of learning model.* Alexandria, VA: ASCD.

McCune, S. D. (1986). *Guide to strategic planning for educators.* Alexandria, VA: ASCD.

McTighe, J., & Ferrara, S. (1995). Performance-based assessment in the classroom. *Pennsylvania Educational Leadership, 2*, 4-15.

National Council for Social Studies. (1994). *Expectations of excellence—Curriculum standards for social studies (Executive Summary).* (Available from National Council of Social Studies, 3501 Newark St., NW Washington DC 20016

Oliva, P. F. (1982). *Developing the curriculum.* Boston: Little, Brown.

Schmoker, M. (1996). *Results—The key to continuous improvement.* Alexandria, VA: ASCD.

Wiggins, G. (1989). Teaching to the authentic test. *Educational Leadership, 7*, 41-47.

Bibliography

Alder, F., & Glunk, J. (1995, October). *Linking outcomes, performance tasks and rubrics*. Presentation at Gateway School District, Monroeville, PA.

Alexander, F. (1993). National standards: A new conventional wisdom. *Educational Leadership, 5,* 9-16.

Baker, E. (1993). Questioning the technical quality of performance assessment. *The School Administrator, 11,* 12-16.

Bonstingl, J. J. (1992). *Schools of quality—An introduction to Total Quality Management*. Alexandria, VA: ASCD.

Bracey, G. W. (1993). Testing the test. *The School Administrator, 11,* 8-11.

Brickell, H., & Regina, P. (1988). *Time for curriculum*. Alexandria, VA: National School Boards Association.

Cain, R., & Kenney, P. (1992). A joint vision for classroom assessment. *Mathematics Teacher, 8,* 612-615.

Castner, K., Costella, L., & Hess, S. (1993). Moving from seat time to mastery: One district's system. *Educational Leadership, 1,* 45-50.

Cheek, D. (1993). Plain talk about alternative assessment. *Middle School Journal, 2,* 6-10.

Cohen, D. (1995). What standards for national standards? *Phi Delta Kappan, 10,* 751-757.

Costa, A. L. (1993). How world-class standards will change us. *Educational Leadership, 5,* 50-51.

Eisner, E. W. (1993). Why standards may not improve schools. *Educational Leadership, 5,* 22-23.

Elmore, R., & Fuhrman, S. (Eds.). (1994). *The governance of curriculum*. Alexandria, VA: ASCD.

Foriska, T. J. (1992). Outcome-based education: Will it change Pennsylvania schools? *Pennsylvania Educational Leadership, 1,* 8-10.

Foriska, T. J. (1994). Curriculum development: A design process for clarity. *Pennsylvania Journal of Teacher Leadership, 1,* 16-19.

Foriska, T. J. (1994). Strategic planning: Designing a future for your organization. *Pennsylvania Educational Leadership, 1,* 24-28.

Foriska, T. J. (1996). Transition outcomes: Beyond strategic planning. *Pennsylvania Educational Leadership, 1,* 22-29.

Glatthorn, A. (1994). *Developing a quality curriculum*. Alexandria, VA: ASCD.

Hofmeister, A., & Lubke, M. (1990). *Research into practice—Implementing effective teaching strategies*. Boston: Allyn & Bacon.

Jasmie, J. (1993). *Portfolios and other assessments*. Huntington Beach, CA: Teacher Created Materials.

Jennings, J. F. (1995). School reform based on what is taught and learned. *Phi Delta Kappan, 10*, 765-769.

Jorgensen, M. (1993). The promise of alternative assessment. *The School Administrator, 11*, 17-23.

Keefe, J. W. (1988). *Profiling and utilizing learning skills*. Alexandria, VA: National Association of Secondary School Principals.

Lewis, A. C. (1995). An overview of the standards movement. *Phi Delta Kappan, 10*, 744-750.

O'Neil, J. (1992). Putting performance assessment to the test. *Educational Leadership, 8*, 14-19.

O'Neil, J. (1993). Can national standards make a difference. *Educational Leadership, 5*, 4-8.

Ott, J. (1994). *Alternative assessment in the mathematics classroom*. New York: Macmillan/McGraw-Hill.

Pate, P., Homestead, E., & McGinnis, K. (1993). Designing rubrics for authentic assessment. *Middle School Journal, 2*, 25-27.

Pellegrini, M. (1990, November 25). Legislators ask for reform in public education. *Pittsburgh Post Gazette*.

Pennsylvania State Education Association. (1993). *Restructuring to promote learning in America's schools—A guidebook*. Harrisburg, PA: Author.

Powell, J. C. (1993). What does it mean to have authentic assessment. *Middle School Journal, 2*, 36-42.

Reed, L. (1993). Achieving the aims and purposes of schooling through authentic assessment. *Middle School Journal, 2*, 11-13.

Rothman, R. (1996). Linking standards and instruction—HELPS is on the way. *Educational Leadership, 8*, 44-46.

Saylor, J., Alexander, W., & Lewis, A. C. (1981). *Curriculum planning for better teaching and learning*. New York: Holt, Rinehart & Winston.

Simmons, R. (1994). The horse before the cart: Assessing for understanding. *Educational Leadership, 5*, 22-23.

Simmons, R., & Resnick, L. (1993). Assessment as the catalyst of school reform. *Educational Leadership, 5*, 11-16.

Sizer, T., & Rogers, B. (1993). Designing standards: Achieving the delicate balance. *Educational Leadership, 5*, 24-26.

Standards and Assessment Task Force. (1994). *Content standards and assessment guide for school physical education*. Alexandria, VA: National Association for Sport and Physical Education.

Steffy, B. (1993). Top-down—bottom-up: Systemic change in Kentucky. *Educational Leadership, 1*, 42-44.

Tinsley, C. (1993). Putting first things first: Changing our assessment practices. *Middle School Journal, 2*, 51-54.

Wiggins, G. (1991). Standards, not standardization: Evoking quality student work. *Educational Leadership, 5*, 18-25.

Wiggins, G. (1992). Creating tests worth taking. *Educational Leadership, 8*, 26-33.

Index

CORWIN
PRESS

The Corwin Press logo—a raven striding across an open book—represents the happy union of courage and learning. We are a professional-level publisher of books and journals for K–12 educators, and we are committed to creating and providing resources that embody these qualities. Corwin's motto is "Success for All Learners."